DADDY'S DYING

THERE IS NO WILL

Charlotte Reece Brown

ISBN 978-1-63814-930-9 (Paperback)
ISBN 978-1-63814-931-6 (Digital)

Covenant Books, Inc.
11661 Hwy 707
Murrells Inlet, SC 29576
www.covenantbooks.com

WESLEY

Father is dying of cancer (in the natural sense). However, life killed him long ago.

Wesley was born to sharecroppers, Clarence and Liz, in a small town called Wild Bottom Creek just outside of Still Hill, Oklahoma. It was December 1930; he was the third son of a family who could not afford their firstborn child. Life was hard from the beginning as Wesley had little food, education, or excitement during his childhood. In the winter, children were required to help with the family farm. Therefore, education was put on the backburner for most during those days. During Christmas, there were few gifts for the children, except for items Liz may receive from her employer. Liz was a cook. She worked in white people's houses, and the family farm to make ends meet. At times, Liz's employer allowed her to take leftover food home to her children. It wasn't much, but the family was grateful.

One December morning 1937, Clarence was walking down the street in Tulsa, Oklahoma, and saw two men fighting. He attempted to stop the fight and was shot in the neck and died, leaving Liz and the children to fend for themselves. As word spread through the town that Clarence died, an older man living in the city known as Mister became interested in Liz and decided to take her as his wife. Liz had no other choice than to be with Mister. She needed someone to help raise her young sons. She thought he was the person to do just that. However, Mister had no heart; he was brutal to Liz as well as the children. Mister was not interested in a wife or family. He needed a maid and someone to work the fields and to tend to the chickens. So Wesley found a way out of this horrible situation. After completing the tenth grade, he joined the army 1948. He felt free from bondage at home while serving in the army for two years. Upon discharge, Wesley called home to tell Liz about his honorable discharge, but he called collect and Mister would not accept the charges. No one could figure out why the family had a phone because no one other than Mister could use it. If the phone rang at Mister's house, he was going to answer it and decide if the call was worth taking.

The army was a good fit for Wesley. He became a brick mason while serving in the army. That's what young black men did in those days. Some finished high school and enlisted. However, since a high school diploma was not required to enter the army, the military was a way out for Wesley. He needed a vocation and the influence of individuals who were not trying to demean or harm him. Wesley experienced racial discrimination in the army. However, being treated unfavorably because of your ethnicity was minuscule compared to the abuse he and his brothers endured while living with Mister.

WESLEY MEETS DESIREE

After being discharged from the army, Wesley worked as a police officer for a short stint. Later, he became a cab driver; that's how he met Desiree. She was divorced with children in tow. They met in 1950, and after dating for two years, Desiree and Wesley married.

In 1952, Wesley and Desiree moved to California to make a better life for their family. The plan was to find jobs in Los Angeles and eventually move the rest of the family to California to start a new life. During the transition, Desiree decided to leave her son and daughter with Aunt Lea. Desiree was gone so long her children did not recognize her when she returned. They believed Aunt Lea was their mom. After being left in an orphanage for a period with minimal explanation, Desiree may have assumed leaving children behind was optional. Flo moved to California, and Liz followed. Desiree introduced Wesley to the church. Her mother Flo was starch religious and allowed no one to separate her from Desiree. If Wesley really wanted to be with Desiree and accepted into the family, he had to get saved or their relationship would end. So he became a member of the church, and not long afterward, Wesley received a call from on high; he became a preacher. They became members of the same church. However, Wesley's mother Liz was Baptist and did not follow the others to the Pentecostal Church.

In 1953, Desiree returned to Tulsa to get her children. Once reunited with Wesley, they started a new family. Wesley and Desiree had one child together and formed a family who struggled forty years to endure one another. Night after night the house was filled with arguments, but that did not stop them from attending church. Charlie wonders how she graduated from high school. Guess it was the nature of things for little black children to pass from one grade to another even if the learning experience was void of helping to develop their minds. The family spent a lot of time in church; however, the household was in shambles. They opened the church doors and closed it literally. Wesley had a key to the church and was dedicated to serving the church and God and demonstrated his devotion by attending every church service. In those days, no one was concerned with children having homework or if they had breakfast or lunch money each day. The focus of life for this family was serving God through physical demonstration of one's sincerity.

The basis of most arguments in the house centered around Wesley and Desiree's unhappy relationship trying to determine who was in charge of the family. Desiree wanted to honor Flo's rules, but couldn't figure out how to balance her role as wife and grown daughter. Wesley also wanted respect and for Iverson and Ruth to think of him as their dad. But Flo intervened, stating that "Iverson and Ruth aren't your children. They don't have to listen to you." So the arguments continued.

Flo eventually moved in and took over their home. She set the rules and Desiree and Wesley followed. That was until Wesley got fed up with Flo's interference. He became the man of the house and ordered Desiree and Liz to call him Rev. Reiss. Initially Desiree refused, but later relented and started calling him Rev. Reiss most of the time. The children were confused; they saw one lifestyle at home and another at church. There were plenty of arguments (almost daily). With both mother-in-laws in and out of the house and interfering in the family affairs, there could be nothing but chaos.

HOME WITH MOM AND DAD

The first memories of life with Wesley and Desiree is living in California in a small two-bedroom house. Charlie was three years old; she can't remember the name of the street they lived on, but they had a place to live and food on the table. Desiree loved parakeets. She had two, one was yellow and the other one had red feathers. The birds would sing and keep up noise during the day. But at night, once Desiree placed a sheet over the birdcage, they were quiet. The birds fascinated Charlie. She wanted them to be her friends, so one day, Charlie let them out of the cage so they could play together. Well, that was a mistake; before she realized it, the birds flew out of an open window.

Charlie remembers helping put up some curtains Desiree made by hand. Charlie was playing with a metal curtain rod. Desiree told her not to play with the curtain rod because she could cut herself. Long story short, she has a scar on her right index finger to show for it. Desiree was talented in sewing, singing, and playing the piano just to name a few of her talents. She also made plastic flowers from newspaper and starch to display in the house. Some of those talents were passed down to Charlie. She could play the piano, organ, and tambourine as well.

Charlie recalled spending time with Wesley as the young man pursued his vocation. He worked nights and took care of her during the day while Desiree worked. Wesley attended Life Bible College, and obtained a certificate of completion in theological studies. The college experience impacted Wesley and enhanced his career path. He was associated with other religious scholars. Wesley created some lifelong friendships in that setting.

CHRISTMAS

Charlie does not want to paint such a dismal depiction of her family; they had good times as well. Wesley worked at Little Debbie's Bakery for a while. They allowed him to bring home leftover stock (items that did not sale). They kept the treats on top of the refrigerator (along with the cereal). Charlie is sure the treats were kept on top of the refrigerator to keep the children from getting into the snacks without permission. During this period, the family seemed better; that's probably because Flo finally moved out and into her own apartment, and Liz found a job with live-in quarters.

Christmas 1963 was great; Desiree cooked all of the family favorites. The family ate until their sides were about to burst. But there was one item they could not touch until Wesley had his giant-sized portion first. The peach cobbler was the main dessert and it was Wesley's favorite. Christmas 1963 is particularly vivid. While the children were supposed to be outside riding their new bikes and playing with the neighborhood children, Iverson kept running in and out of the house. Oh yeah, Iverson is Charlie's older brother from another father. Desiree heard the back door slam several times; she told Iverson that Wesley was asleep and to stay outside until she called for them to come inside. Truth is Wesley worked nights and to have their alone time, the parents allowed their children to play outside for long periods. The children did not think anything of it, they never thought about Desiree and Wesley spending quality time together or having sex. Who knew?

Eventually, Desiree called for the children to come inside; her voice sounded different. She was angry and immediately starting questioning them about the peach cobbler that disappeared from the stovetop while they were playing outside. Desiree started the speech about loving them and wanting the children to be good and to tell her the truth about the cobbler. Ruth and Charlie started crying and told Desiree that they did not know what happened to the cobbler. On the other hand, Iverson told Desiree that he loved her and that when he grows up, he would buy her diamonds and a car. Desiree wanted to know why Iverson was making promises. She asked him once more, "Did you eat the cobbler?" Iverson lied and said, "No, ma'am," and Desiree started beating him with a leather belt. Well, Iverson couldn't keep it to himself. As she beat him, he started throwing up. It was clear to see, his stomach was filled with peach cobbler. Caught red-handed and bugging out with red eyes and beads of sweat running down his face, Iverson did not have to say another word. He could not deny eating the peach cobbler.

During Iverson's beating, the sisters were kneeling in front of the couch with their dresses pulled tight around their butts in case Desiree needed to whip them as well. That was the position they took during punishments. The girls were crying their eyes out and praying to God for forgiveness even though they were not guilty. Later they found out each time Iverson went in and out of the house, he ate some the cobbler and eventually half of the dessert was gone. Thank God the beating finally stopped; the sisters went back outside. They were not sure if anything else happened to Iverson that day. Somehow, they all lived through it.

OKLAHOMA, WHERE THE...

The family lived in Watts a suburb of Los Angeles, California, this was before the LA riots between 1961 to 1963. They had a nice house with three bedrooms. But it did not last long. Before they knew it, the family moved to another apartment across the street from an elementary school on Ninety-Second Street. Not long after moving into the apartment, the family was told, "God has called me to the ministry back in Oklahoma." The family is moving to Tulsa so Wesley could pursue his ministry. Iverson and Ruth were in the eleventh and twelfth grade respectively. They did not want to move; Iverson was on the track team and played football. Charlie's sister was a dancer, she could sing. They had big plans and wanted to stay in Los Angeles no matter what.

Wesley and Desiree did not allow them to stay in Los Angeles; in 1964, they moved the family to Tulsa, Oklahoma, and things went downhill from there. Wesley followed Liz back to Tulsa. She moved back some months before Wesley made his big announcement. Upon arrival in Tulsa, they moved in with Liz. She had a small three-bedroom home. She allowed them to move in, thinking it was short-term. They lived with Liz until Charlie went to the tenth grade, so from 1964 to 1969, Liz shared her house with the family. Iverson left home at sixteen to live with Aunt Lea. She allowed him to smoke cigarettes and drink alcohol. That's how he wanted to live. Once Iverson moved, the rules laid down by Wesley no longer applied. Ruth got married as soon as possible. And Charlie was left alone with three crazy adults. Iverson eventually went to the army; Ruth moved to

Kansas and started a family. The parents stayed together working in the church and running revivals when Wesley wasn't working construction jobs.

Ultimately, Wesley stopped working construction and started working for his pastor nicknamed Preacher. Preacher was one of the meanest men Charlie ever knew. He was cruel and seemed to hate everyone including his wife. When contractors finished building new homes, Preacher and crew would perform the finishing touches on the homes. They would clean the homes by removing paint and concrete from the windows and clean the inside to make the homes ready for occupancy. Preacher did not pay his employees consistently. Friday would roll around and once again, no paycheck for Wesley. At least that's the story they were told. Wesley wasn't a lazy person, so Charlie believed the scenario. When he got paid, the family knew what dinner would consist of. There is a hamburger stand in Tulsa called Lot-A-Burger. It was a hamburger place; you'd walk up, put your order in through the tiny window covered with grease stains from hamburgers and French fires being cooked. You'd get back in your car and wait until your order number was called over the loud-speaker. Now the place is brick and mortar, still cranking out those burgers.

The church was the focus of the family. Wesley started numerous churches, but never experienced growth or church expansion. The state presiding bishop would contact Wesley with church assignments for congregations without a pastor. He continued to take church assignments and wanted to become a bishop. As fate would have it, Wesley worked his fingers to the bone for the church. He gave his last dime in the offerings knowing that the family had nothing to eat at home. He thought it was better to give than receive. Wesley was unsuccessful as a pastor because of the lifestyle he lived, coupled with his dysfunctional family at home. Any disturbance between the couple was easily known because they would sometimes argue in public. At that point, Desiree would display emotional outburst that could not be ignored. Wesley seemed unconcerned or embarrassed to be seen and heard arguing with his wife in public. Wesley and Desiree's marriage lacked the foundation of a true love affair. They may have married too soon and were not knowledgeable about family and married life.

The church officials liked Wesley because he could motivate parishioners into giving money, resulting in large offerings during state church meetings. Other than raising offerings they did not allow him to do much more. But Wesley never gave up even when he became ill with cancer. That is until Wesley and Desiree escaped from Tulsa by moving to Dallas, Texas.

WHEN WE KNOW BETTER, WE DO BETTER

D esiree believed in God and was saved. She devoted herself to being Flo's daughter and working in the church. After all, we do what we see, not so much of what we are taught. Flo managed her life in the same manner. Although both ladies were saved and filled with the Holy Ghost, they were not exposed to work-life balance. Both played the piano and were evangelist/missionaries in the COGIC world. However, they experienced turbulent marriages. Flo and Desiree did not know about domestic violence, and self-help books probably wouldn't be read by either. The old adage was "If you don't like something, change it. If you can't change it, change your attitude" (Maya Angelou). Desiree chose the latter; she still talks about Rev. Reiss today.

Wesley was sick, but his children did not know it. The parents were good at hiding the truth from the family. However, this time they couldn't keep the secret much longer. The cancer took over; during this period, Wesley explained the conditions of the marriage and how he felt about Iverson and Ruth. They were his stepchildren. For forty years, he tried to be a father to them, but with interference from both mother-in-laws and his personal feelings about rearing someone else's children as his own, he felt like a failure. He never felt accepted as their father. Wesley died inside long before the cancer diagnoses.

Charlie was young and did not understand why people treated her different from her brother and sister. Charlie believed her siblings disliked her because of it. They couldn't help it after being mistreated for so long. Charlie listened to her father and finally understood his point of view. She realized he was human and subject to mistakes. And Desiree should have been treated better during the formative years. During the winter of 1970, Wesley attempted suicide. He started the car in the garage, but did not raise the garage door. Desiree found him passed out slumped over behind the steering wheel. She called for help. He was sick and depressed. Eventually, he was on Prozac and numerous medications trying to deal with the struggles of everyday life.

AUNT WILLA

Desiree had a friend called Aunt Willa. She had a nice house, and she could cook. She baked pies and cakes for the church and she fed Charlie and Ruth on numerous occasions. Aunt Willa's house wasn't far from where Charlie lived, so they walked to her house almost daily. She always had something cooking on the stove. Aunt Willa was married but did not have any children, so she enjoyed the time the sisters spent with her. One day while visiting Aunt Willa, Charlie noticed Aunt Willa's dog was bleeding. She did not know what was wrong with the dog, so Charlie told Aunt Willa her dog was sick and needed to see a doctor. Well, the dog wasn't sick. She was on her monthly cycle otherwise known as being in heat. That's how Charlie learned that women menstruate.

Aunt Willa calmly explained what was happening with the dog. She also told Charlie about women experiencing the same thing and that she may have this happen one day. Aunt Willa's husband owned hogs. One day, Aunt Willa and her husband took the children to the hog farm to watch them slaughter hogs. Charlie remembered someone using the hog's blood to make a blood pie. She stayed far away from that pie. They spent the entire day on the farm. The day was peaceful, no arguments or the sound of slamming doors. No screaming or cursing. One day, Aunt Willa's husband died. For some reason after his death, the family did not hear much from her. However, she had an impact on the sisters' lives and taught Charlie and Ruth about cooking and taking care of a family. She was like a grandmother to the sisters.

CHURCH

During Sunday morning church service, the building was packed. The pastor, Bishop Leland, preached his heart out and the saints couldn't contain themselves. Desiree was the church pianist. She starting playing a fast congregational song, Charlie picked up her tambourine and started to play. The church was in an uproar, as different people danced across the dusty wooden floors. The spirit was high as some people came to the altar to get saved. Some came to get filled with the Holy Ghost. And others came just to feel the supernatural power of God which flowed from one individual to another.

Charlie was a child, but she could feel the spirit of the Lord that day. She was only six years old, but was anointed to play the tambourine and could compete with most of the older children in keeping up with the fast tempo of the music. The natural talent of playing the tambourine comes from her father who played the drums as a young man.

As the tempo of the music picked up, the building started to give way to the vibrations. One of the deacons sitting in the deacon section of the church beneath a wood-framed window began praising God from his chair and feeling the Holy Ghost. He never moved from his chair, but stomped his feet and clapped his hands to the music; you could see the dust rise from the wooden floor as he stomped his feet and became more excited. Suddenly the window above his head became unhinged and fell on him, the glass shattered and the frame of the window made circles around the deacon's neck. As the window shattered, the deacon continued to praise God, and the saints danced until some passed out in the aisles of the church.

There were no cuts, bruises or any marks on this man. God put his shield of protection on the deacon as a sign of His Power and Glory. The ushers could not find enough materials to cover the women who passed out under the power of the Holy Ghost, so they made human shields around them to keep men from seeing undergarments and other unmentionables.

When church was over, the children couldn't wait to get home to tell Liz the events of the day. Once at home, they told Liz everything that happened, but saved the best for last. While explaining what happened to the deacon, Liz began to laugh. When she laughed, her front teeth flew from her mouth and landed across the room. Charlie was in shock; her siblings left her standing in front of Liz, rocking back and forth as if she was sitting in a rocking chair. She continued to look up at Liz in amazement. Charlie slowly excused herself and found Iverson to ask what happened to Liz's front teeth. This was the day Charlie learned about false teeth. And still today, false teeth give her the creeps.

GRANDMOTHERS

Flo, Desiree's mother, had false teeth as well. Her false teeth were kept in a small glass of water on the nightstand next to her bed. Charlie wouldn't go into Flo's bedroom if those teeth were there. Flo played the piano and sang solos during church. One Sunday night, it was time for the altar call. This was the sacred portion of the church service. Everyone had to be quiet, and no one should be walking during the altar call. Flo began to play the piano and singing. She opened her mouth wide to hit a high note; her false teeth flew from her mouth and bounced on the piano. Flo reached out, grabbed her teeth, placed them back in her mouth, and continued the song. She did not miss a note or beat. However, the children in the choir-stand lost it. They snickered and laughed until the pastor looked at the children with an expression and look in his eyes that would stop traffic, let alone stop a few children from misbehaving. Flo was most upset with Iverson, not sure why, but she took her anger out by fussing at him for making fun of her mishap during church services. She couldn't fuss at Charlie because Wesley was her father, and he would not allow it.

Flo and Wesley did not get along; she did not like Charlie and did not show any affection toward her. She was Charlie's grandmother, but did not love her. Charlie was afraid of her because she liked to beat children. It seems like Flo would spank a child just for the fun of it. At least that's what it seemed like to Charlie.

Any infraction no matter how small, if she could get her hands on you, she would punish you in some fashion. One form of punishment was to have a child face the corner of any room, stand on one foot with both hands on their heads for long periods. If you fell down or your foot slipped, the punishment phase would start again.

However, Flo knew how to entertain children with games she made up. For example, she made up a game called Tops. Flo kept a collection of pop bottle tops as game pieces. To start the game, Flo would turn the pop bottle tops face down on a table or on the floor and mix them up as if she were stirring a pot soup, then pull two pop bottle tops and turn them over. To be the winner of the game, one had to pull three identical sets of pop bottle tops. Two Pepsi, Coke, and Bubble up bottle tops pulled during the game and you were the winner. Any number of people could play similar to playing dominoes or cards.

Flo treated her daughters differently. She loved Desiree and treated Lea like a maid. If she needed something done like cooking, cleaning, or anything domestic, Lea was in the limelight. But for show, Desiree was the star. She could sing play the piano and knew how to dress and do hair. Flo considered one light skinned and the other was dark and dumb. In Black society, light skinned verses dark skinned exist. Some use the misnomer to declare one person as beautiful and smart, as opposed to those lacking the aforementioned.

Liz was a cook and housekeeper. She found work in Hollywood, Charlie's not sure if she worked for any famous people. But the people she worked for were rich and had two little boys. Liz worked by cooking, cleaning, and taking care of their children. She lived in the servant's quarters during the week, and on weekends, she would visit with Charlie's family. Liz had another son DD who lived in LA; he had ten children and a wife who hated Liz. When Liz was a young woman, she had an affair with an older man who turned out to be DD's father-in-law. Liz had a baby by the father-in-law. Once DD's wife heard that information, she vowed to hate Liz for the rest of her natural life. Liz allowed her barren sister to raise the little girl fathered by DD's father-in-law.

Liz was the mother of five sons. One of her son's died in a drowning accident when he was eight years old. The other two had lives of their own, one lived in Utah and the other son lived and worked in Memphis, Tennessee. Both sons had families and made good lives for themselves. However, none of them were as close to Liz as Wesley. They always lived with one another or in close proximity of each other.

With help from Flo and Liz, Charlie's family was dysfunctional and did not show love and respect toward one another. Wesley wanted to adopt Iverson and his sister. Instead of someone telling a seven- and six-year-old what was about to happen. Someone asked Iverson what he wanted: do you want to change your last name to Reiss or keep the name you were born with? The seven-year-old decided to keep his name, so his sister did the same.

Liz had a habit of introducing the children as "This is Iverson and his sister, you know they aren't Wesley's but this one is," pointing to Charlie. One day, Iverson asked Desiree why Liz kept saying that Wesley wasn't his dad. Flo was happy to explain that Desiree had them by a different man and that Wesley was not their natural father. From that point on, the family was split, Iverson and Ruth against Wesley with Desiree in the middle as referee. Charlie blamed Wesley and Desiree for allowing Flo and Liz to takeover by making decisions for and about the family. The family was none of their business. And Desiree just sat there and let Flo do and say whatever she wanted. Wesley saw the situation blossoming into a forbidden, smelly, unattractive weed, but did nothing to nip the situation in the bud.

That's what old people did in those days. There was no TV or telephone, and all Liz and Flo had for entertainment was Charlie and her family. Flo and Liz had other agents in making sure the family failed. Their cousins and friends of the family kept the weed of deceit growing. They were sure to show affection and concern toward Charlie, but left Iverson and his sister in the cold. These people gushed over Charlie and did not know her. All they saw was a little black girl who happened to favor Wesley. "Oh, this is Iverson and his sister. They aren't Wesley's, but this one is." Over and over, this statement was heard. Sometimes the children would mouth the words as Liz spoke, "They aren't Wesley's."

MY BIRTHDAY

Liz organized a large birthday party for Charlie's fourth birthday. The party was held at a cafeteria in Huntington Beach, California. The room was decorated in pink and white, with tables assembled in a U-shape. White tablecloths draped the tables. Each child presented gifts wrapped in beautiful wrapping paper fastened with colorful ribbons. *All those gifts were for me?* Charlie thought. She couldn't believe it. Charlie saw people she had never met before, and the worst part was Iverson and his sister were not invited. Charlie thought Liz was taking her on a shopping trip. They rode the bus from Watts to Huntington Beach. When they arrived and got off the bus, Charlie was ready to shop. But Liz said she had a surprise for her. They entered a cafeteria and went into a large room full of unfamiliar faces. Charlie tried to asked why the rest of her family wasn't there, but Liz assured Charlie that everything was okay and to just have fun.

Each gift was in a box, and each box contained wrapping tissue with beautiful underwear inside. Charlie received numerous pairs of underwear (panties with flower and balloons) and long white bobbysocks. She was impressed and excited, and soon forgot about Iverson and her sister. Charlie loved the attention and thought she was queen for a day. *Queen for a Day* was one of the highly rated game shows that came on TV at the time. They watched the show while visiting Uncle DD's house.

As one may imagine the story of her birthday party was difficult to recall. Her brother and sister were not in attendance, and they were not invited to the party. Wesley and Desiree knew, but did nothing. Once again, Liz reinforced the fact that Iverson and Ruth were not her grandchildren. This is just one example of how family members meddled in the family affairs. Wesley and Desiree were not sure how their family should be managed and who had the final say about their children's welfare.

DISNEYLAND

Two of Charlie's cousins came from Utah for the summer of 1963. The family took them to Disneyland. The price to get into Disneyland was $3.95 for child and $4.95 per adult. Uncle DD could pay for his large family to get into the park because he worked for the railroad and his retirement from the military. They had a blast. But everyone ended up sick. Like numbskulls, they ate and immediately rode the cup and saucer ride. They went around and around, colors changed as the cup and saucer ride moved round and round. One by one, they fell like flies under a spell from a witches' brew. Everyone was nauseated and throwing up.

Liz couldn't allow the trip to end without throwing a wrench into the mix. She took the children shopping. Iverson, Ruth, and Charlie went along with the cousins from Utah. Liz purchased several winter coats. She gave the cousins one each, but when it came to Iverson and Ruth, Liz promised to take care of them later. She purchased a car coat for Charlie which was fashionable during that time. The coat was short and had a hood with fake fur trim. Charlie was young and thrilled that she had a new coat, she did not realize what had taken place with Iverson and Ruth until they complained to Desiree. The cousins boarded a Greyhound bus bound for Utah. Liz brought Iverson, Ruth, and Charlie back home. Liz eventually returned to her job in Hollywood, leaving yet another situation for Desiree to explain to Iverson and Ruth.

During one of Liz's weekend visits, she gave Charlie a pair of skates. The skates were plastic, pink and blue in color. The skates fit over your shoes and then fastened around your ankle with Velcro strip. Charlie was having problems getting the skates to stay on her shoes. So one of those words she learned from Liz slipped out. She shouted "shit" and threw the skates across the porch when they wouldn't stay on. Well, Iverson heard Charlie say the forbidden and so did Liz. That was the only time she punished Charlie. Liz actually spanked Charlie, but ended up in tears herself. She did not want to hurt her favorite granddaughter.

She spanked Charlie and told her that nice little girls don't use bad language. However, she never explained that nice old ladies could. Liz was a Christian and loved God for sure. But some of the things she said and did were unforgivable. Charlie was ten years old and remembers sitting in her living room as Liz talked on the phone with the pastor's wife about Desiree. Liz said that Desiree acts like she lost her mind. She went on to say that Desiree was screaming and crying for no reason, but she forgot Charlie was in the room. Charlie was mad that someone she loved, that she was sure loved her would talk about Desiree that way. Charlie spoke up and told Liz, "Don't ever talk about my mother again." Liz was shocked and couldn't believe Charlie was paying attention to her conversation. Charlie wasn't eavesdropping; Liz was talking so loudly she couldn't help but hear what Liz was saying. Liz huffed and started praying and rocking back and forth in her chair.

Quietness kept; Desiree showed signs of dementia early in life. We did not understand why she acted out, screamed, and cried for no apparent reason. If Desiree wanted to cause a commotion, she could. And no one tried to stop it or figure out what was happening. Well, back in those days, people did not know about dementia. It was called senility. But Desiree was too young for that diagnosis; dementia is a brain disease that causes a long-term and often gradual decrease in the ability to think and function in daily activities. However, during that time, the family was not aware of the disease.

One funny story about Liz comes to mind. When Charlie and her family moved from Los Angeles to Tulsa, they learned that Liz had a lover. Mr. Pigg was her insurance man, they had sex and made noises while making love. One evening, the family returned from church a little early. The front door wasn't locked, but the safety chain was on the door. Charlie turned the key in the lock, pushed against the front door; they saw butts and heard Liz say, "Ooh, ooh like, this is good to me." Initially, they did not hear the family at the door, but eventually they got up and ran into the bathroom for cover. The family was embarrassed, but they laughed. However, Wesley did not know how to handle the situation. Liz managed to save face and pretended nothing happened.

MISSIONARY FLO

Charlie never knew Flo to have a man friend, but was sure she did. After all, Flo had two daughters. But the Flo the family knew, one wouldn't think she ever had sex or was involved with a man outside of the church. It turns out Desiree and Lea had different fathers. Flo was married to Lea's dad, but it's unclear if she was married to Desiree's father. Charlie was a grown woman before learning that Flo had an affair with her pastor when she was a young missionary in the church. She passed the child off as being by a previous husband, but everyone knew that wasn't true.

While living in a small country town outside of Tulsa, Flo worked in the church; however, she became an unwed mother. Charlie believed that's why she had so many rules. She would not allow the girls to wear pants, fingernail polish, or any type of makeup. She did not want boys to visit the home and none of them could talk on the phone. As Ruth matured, she got permission for one of her boyfriends to visit the home. They tried to talk to each other, but Flo stayed in the room and listened to everything that was going on. Flo went into the kitchen, she returned to see Ruth sitting too close to her boyfriend. Flo screamed, "Why don't you get up and sit in his lap?" After that the boy left and Ruth cried herself to sleep.

ZION BAPTIST CHURCH

Even though Liz talked about Desiree, Charlie still followed Liz to church. She wanted to become Baptist. Charlie set her sights on getting into the Baptist church and wanted to get baptized as well. She attended Zion Baptist Church as often as she could get out of going to church with Desiree and Wesley. It did not happen often, but just enough for Charlie to fall in love with the way the old deacons prayed and sang. It was something about the sound of the old men's voices that bellowed to the bowels of the church and back into the sanctuary to those awaiting a touch from the Lord. They would start out with "Father, I Stretch My Hand to Thee," something would come over Charlie. She wanted to be a Baptist; after all, they did not roll around on the floor and speak in tongues like some in the COGIC church. Her classmates knew that Wesley was a Pentecostal preacher. And that Desiree and Flo were missionaries. So for Charlie to become Baptist was a big deal. She had an opportunity to take a picture with Liz's mission group. Charlie was so proud and cherished that glossy 8 ½ × 11 black and white photograph.

MIDDLE CHILD SYNDROME

Ruth is the middle child with all the symptoms of her position in life. Someone is always mistreating her or saying something to upset her day. Her childhood was more difficult than Iverson or Charlie's. Per Ruth, she was a lovable child who never caused a problem. However, Ruth has a fighting spirit. She will fight anyone anywhere, anytime. That fighting spirit comes from Flo, and Ruth is just like Flo in that respect. Some of her ways emulate Flo, even down to Ruth's obsession with whipping children. It doesn't matter who the children belong to, if a child says something or if they do something Ruth doesn't approve of, she will correct the child and their parents if necessary.

Ruth had many lovers and multiple husbands. One of her boyfriends, Johnnie, was in love with Ruth, he wanted to marry her. They dated in high school, during that time Johnnie bought Ruth some clothes and two pairs of shoes. Wesley insisted that Ruth return what Johnnie purchased. Once again, the house was full of loud voices and slamming doors. Desiree did not know what to do or say. She wanted Ruth to have nice things, but the family could not afford it. Johnnie and Ruth eventually broke up, but Charlie thought he would have been a good husband for Ruth. Johnnie was devastated because of the breakup. He left town and joined the Air Force.

Somehow, Charlie became the scapegoat in this scenario. Johnnie's sister (a known prostitute in the city) approached Charlie, saying, "Why did Ruth breakup with my brother Johnnie?" She threatened to beat Charlie up because of Johnnie's heartache. Of course,

Charlie acted tough and ready to fight, but was actually shaking in her boots. This girl was still in middle school, but older than most in the school. She would have been a force to deal with because of her size and stature. She outweighed Charlie by one hundred pounds. And towered over her as well. She was the size of a grown woman. During the argument, the principal approached Charlie from behind while she was talking cursing and defending herself to Johnnie's sister. Both girls were in trouble and received swats from the principal. Charlie didn't think it was fair, and Wesley visited with the principal and advised that he did not agree with his actions. Charlie had to defend herself and thought the older girl should have apologized.

Ruth found a way out by marrying husband number one who was a spoiled brat from Missouri. Ruth insisted that she get married and husband number one seemed to want the marriage as well. However, his mother was a prostitute, with large breasts and a potty mouth. She did not think Ruth was good enough for her son. She had no problem letting her thoughts be known. Ruth married husband number one anyway.

The marriage was bad from the start as he watched everything she did. This guy marked the milk and bread containers so he would know if other people were eating his food while he was out of the house. Ruth tried to make the marriage work but finally gave up. Husband number one was a jerk; however, she had one child with him. She tried to convince husband number one that a second child was his, but it did not work. She had an affair with the neighbor who lived with his mother in a two-bedroom apartment across the hall. Ruth left the marriage because of infidelities by both herself and husband number one. She eventually moved back into Desiree and Wesley's house.

They lived in a nice place with plenty of room. The back porch was wide enough to put Desiree's piano on, so she could practice whenever she wanted without waking Wesley up. One summer day, Wesley and Desiree were at work. Ruth had her boyfriend come over. She instructed him to come to the back door so Charlie wouldn't know what was going on. Well, Charlie played the piano as well and wanted to play while her parents were out of the house. The back door leading into the kitchen had a hook latch on it, but it shouldn't have been locked, as no one else was in the house expect Charlie and Ruth.

When Charlie attempted to open the back door, the hook latch was on. But the door opened wide enough to see unmentionables down around her ankles. Charlie heard scooting and shuffling about. She insisted the door be opened up. Ruth told her to go back to her room and leave her alone. But Charlie was thirteen, just old enough to know something was happening that shouldn't have taken place in her parents' house. She saw the boyfriend running from the back porch around the side of the house. So Charlie knew who he was and what Ruth was up to. Ruth always had a repetition of fighting, and she thought Charlie was afraid of her. At the age of thirteen, Charlie was as big and tall as Ruth. She grabbed one of her walking dolls, pulled the leg off, and told Ruth to come on and dared Ruth to hit her.

A walking doll was about three and a half feet tall, if you pulled her left arm, she would take a step or two. Charlie collected dolls and had plenty of dolls to choose from. Ruth threatened her, but never touched her. Charlie called Desiree and told her what happened. She is not sure if Desiree pursued the situation, but that subject was never mentioned again in Charlie's presence. Ruth went on to be with several other guys; husband number two was abusive. He hurt Ruth's oldest child, so she left him and moved back in with Wesley and Desiree. The next guy became husband number three; he was into the Hollywood lifestyle. He worked as a bouncer. So Ruth was in heaven getting to meet and party with celebrities.

HIGH LIFE

During senior year in high school, Ruth thought Charlie should go out to a nightclub. Charlie was excited to go, Ruth had nice party clothes, shoes, and wigs. She loaned Charlie a pantsuit to wear. She was supposed to go home because the next day was Sunday and Charlie had to go to church. But she went to the club and danced to the wee hours of the night. When they returned to Ruth's apartment, Wesley was there. He did not say anything to them, he just motioned to Charlie to get into his car. He did not talk to her during the ride home. Charlie knew he was mad at her for going and at Ruth for taking his child into a den of iniquity.

COLLEGE

Charlie could not wait to leave home under the guise of going to college to get an education. She partied and drank and did a few other unmentionable things. Charlie and her best friend were room-mates in college. However, they had different agendas. While she studied and pledged sorority, Charlie went to every party on campus. Oh yeah, Charlie went to class, but that was not her priority. During one of the campus parties, she met a guy named Lee, he was tall, handsome, and pretended to be shy. She noticed him and told her best friend, "I'm going to talk to him if it's the last thing I ever do." Charlie smoked Salem Lights cigarettes, so she pretended to need a light for her cigarette.

Charlie spoke to the tall handsome guy and asked if he had a light. In those days, most people smoked if for no other reason than to look cool while having a drink or picking up someone for the night. Charlie introduced herself to Lee, he gave her a light for the cigarette and they talked for a while. Charlie couldn't believe a tall good-looking man like Lee was interested in her.

Charlie saw Lee on campus the next few days, and each time they met up, he had a large book underneath his arm. Charlie asked, "Are you studying again?" He smiled and answered yes. They chatted and eventually started seeing one another on a regular basis. However, they did not discuss whether they were exclusive or not. No mention of "will you go with me" or "do you like me" came up. It felt natural, and Charlie was impressed with an upperclassman showing interest in her, a freshman.

There was a dance scheduled for homecoming weekend. Charlie and Lee decided to go to the dance together. As a favor, Charlie brought a girl to the party, so Lee's best friend Porter would not be lonely. It was not a blind date, but those two were supposed to be company for one another. Charlie and Lee danced the night away, Charlie in her sequenced black jacket, wig tight, and high heel shoes. Lee wore a black outfit and platform shoes. Platform shoes were a big deal in those days. The guys would get extra shoe soles and heels stacked on shoes so they would appear taller. The shoeshine man would alter shoe to fit the personality. So black shoes with gold trim fit the bill for the night.

CLICK YOUR HEELS
THREE TIMES

Lee and Charlie dated and eventually moved in together. It was official, they were married in a Baptist church and Charlie became a Baptist that day. She dropped out of college and started working in a hospital as a dietary helper. After a few months of marriage, Lee finished college, got a job in Kansas; they moved and started a new life together. The first few months in Kansas were difficult, but after the checks from Lee's jobs started rolling in and Charlie found employment, they were set. Charlie and Lee lived in a townhome; however, in those days no one heard the word "townhome," it was an apartment with three levels. They had a kitchen, living room, upstairs two small bedrooms with the bathroom in the hallway. There was a basement where they did laundry and grew marijuana plants. The plants grew four feet high. Later, Charlie thought they were so stupid growing that junk in their home. They never thought about getting busted. During the '70s, it was not dangerous being involved with drugs. They frequented clubs where people shared marijuana, it was no big deal, no one thought about germs or disease. It was habit forming but inexpensive.

Charlie was home alone and had partaken in a few hits of marijuana. Someone knocked on the door, and she opened it and found three women from the church of "I know you need to be saved" standing on the porch. Charlie let them in, but forgot they had a pound of marijuana lying on the floor near the couch in full view of these church people. They witnessed to her and asked if she believed in Jesus Christ. She spoke up and said, "Of course I believe in Jesus

Christ, and I know he bled and died for me on the cross." On the inside, she was shaking and waiting for them to stop talking and get out. She was so paranoid she thought they would turn her into the police for having marijuana in their presence.

Although she was grown and married, Charlie longed for the comforts of her father's house. They did not have much; however, she was treated well and was loved. So yes, at times, she wanted to click her heels three times and find herself back home.

PARENTHOOD

Lee and Charlie are the parents of three daughters who are grown and have families of their own. The family is close and supportive. However, they are dysfunctional as well. Charlie never imagined she would have to take on the role of referee between her husband and children. She played the role of peacemaker for a longtime because she always thought her family would be different as opposed to the people she grew up with.

Lee was a great provider and loved his family, but he was hard on their daughters; this action has spilled over into their adult lives. Charlie was the softy in the bunch, striving to make everyone happy while ignoring her own needs at times. She was mother and wife, guardian and the police. Charlie wore herself out tending to family issues. She was trying to make her family something it was resistant to. People are people, and there is nothing she could do to make members of society play the role the way it was written in her dreams.

She thought they would have their children and ride off into the sunset or follow the yellow brink rode to happiness. No way, that did not happen, and she was in a state of utopia, wishing her family was unique.

PARTY OVER HERE!

Charlie turned out to be a party girl, even after her children were born. She couldn't party as a teenager, so she took the opportunity to party most weekends while living in Kansas. Charlie worked Monday through Friday, but on the weekend, she was in the club. She worked with a group of ladies who like to get out as well, so Charlie was in her element. They made up excuses to get out of the house. Charlie did not have to worry who would watch her children, Lee was a homebody and she knew they would be safe with him. Charlie remembers one year during New Year's, she begged Lee to go out to bring in the New Year together. He did not want to go, so she called up her friends and away they went. The ladies went to five different clubs; it was easy because there was no cover charge for women and most of the time guys in the club paid for their drinks. They partied upstairs until 1:00 a.m. and went to the after-party downstairs in the club, and partied there as well. It's laughable, but the ladies took a break by stopping by one of the women's homes. They ended up falling asleep. Charlie woke up at 4:30 a.m. and drove home somehow. Charlie doesn't remember the entire trip because she was drunk and high. The only way she reached home was because God had his hands on her. Charlie arrived at home without getting into an accident or being stopped by the police.

Charlie made it home and went upstairs. She expected Lee would be asleep and not know exactly when she arrived home that morning. Charlie stepped inside the master bedroom, and in the darkness, she noticed a lit cigarette and smoke in the air and realized he was upset and knew she was out all night. Charlie was so out of it, all she could do was lay across the bed and listen to Lee's comments about her behavior. To this day, Charlie was not clear on exactly what

Lee said because she was asleep by the time her head hit the pillow. Charlie continued that lifestyle and enjoyed herself immensely. Maybe that's what happens to children whose parents are strict about every aspect of life. After she was an adult and married, Charlie broke every commandment she knew of (except adultery and murder). Her actions were not malicious or hurtful, but she took every opportunity to do things she could not do as a teenager. Lee was helpful in Charlie's learning experience and encouraged her through most of it. However, he took exception when it came to the nightlife.

DEATH BECOMES HER

It is inevitable, one day we will die. But no one expects to bury a child or younger family member. The family experienced this situation when their great niece who was nineteen at the time was gunned down in cold blood. She was in the wrong place at the wrong time. A maniac took their great niece's life because his girlfriend no longer wanted to be with him. Their great niece was this girl's best friend and the two spent a lot of time together. One day in Tulsa, the maniac found his girlfriend sitting in a truck with the niece and a guy he did not know. They were scheduled to leave for Dallas, but never made it because the maniac shot them to death.

Ultimately, there were three people in the truck, he started with the guy by riddling his body with bullets, then he aimed the gun at his former girlfriend shooting her in the lower torsos, and the great niece was shot in the head and chest. When the smoke cleared, there was silence. The event was over, but gave the appearance of a movie shown in slow motion. The shooter ran, disappearing into the shadows of abandoned homes in North Tulsa. No, Charlie wasn't there, but the information from bystanders and the police report allows her to tell this story as if she witnessed it firsthand. The maniac killed the guy, crippled the former girlfriend, and killed the great niece. He is in jail for life, but that won't bring the great niece back or give the former girlfriend another chance to experience life with someone who may have treated her like a human being instead of a possession. No, Charlie can't give the maniac a name. He is someone who lost their way in society. The police found him hiding in an abandoned crack house. However, he will remain nameless in Charlie's world.

Less than two years later, her niece Mona died of heart failure. Once again, the family was devastated and left wondering if their family could have been more proactive in helping her niece with health issues. She was ill, but the family was unaware. Mona did not tell her own mother about the seriousness of her condition. She dealt with some family issues that left her wanting for a more stable home life. But as life goes, her husband was known for cheating. Yes, he is an adulterer. Mona thought she could change him and started the journey of marriage with the cheater with her eyes wide open. She was the mother of two, one child is mentioned above as she was murdered. And the other child decided to have a sex change and lives as a man called Cleo.

With her nieces dying and leaving the one alone, their family was shattered. Cleo lives in the Bronx and works as a waiter by day and a bouncer at night. Not long after Mona's death, the stepdad remarried again to someone who bears a strong resemblance to Mona. Cleo thought she had a loving relationship with her stepdad and tried to hang on to him, but he wanted nothing to do with Cleo. The stepdad collected the death benefits and moved on with his new wife.

Ruth is Mona's mother; where does she find the strength to make it through the tough times? The larger portion of her family died within a few years of one another. Oh yes, she has other children but can't count on either to step up and become the leader of the family. Everything falls on Ruth's shoulder, and most look to her to resolve issues that may arise. While working through grief and underlying family issues, Ruth went on to become the Retirement Plans Manager for the Phoenix School of Medicine. She accomplished most of her dreams after receiving an appointment as Senior Council to the Head of Van Guard Phoenix. So many accomplishments, but she is still unhappy.

Iverson married Alison, and they became the parent of six sons. Iverson retired from the US Mint, and Alison retired from the Department of Agriculture. They have a few grandchildren but plenty of drama. Iverson and his family lived out of state therefore Charlie does not have much information on their lives. However, her sister-in-law stated that her brother was a good provider and loved his family. He too had demons to deal with; however, he took care of his family.

BACK TO WESLEY

Although Wesley became a preacher, he never let go of one habit. He tried to balance life between drugs and church, going through ups and downs with Desiree and putting up with meddling in-laws. Wesley used marijuana over the years. He kept it from the family, but Charlie found out firsthand because he took ½ lb. of marijuana from her during the '80s. Her Dad came to visit Charlie and her family while living in Kansas. Charlie hid the substance underneath the waterbed. Not sure how he found it, but she knew Wesley took it. He had glaucoma and dealt with it by using marijuana. Charlie never disclosed this information to anyone except her husband, as it was his stash that was lifted from their home. Wesley could have taken a portion of the stash and left the rest. But for some reason, he took the whole bag.

Wesley was a brick mason. When the Midwest weather allowed, he worked construction assignments throughout Oklahoma and Texas. During one assignment, Wesley suffered a debilitating injury requiring physical therapy. Wesley neglected to tell the doctors about his propensity toward drug abuse. Between the pain meds, marijuana mixed with other substances Wesley lived a double life. On one hand, he was the upright straight-laced preacher, and on the other he was addicted to pain meds. She hates putting Wesley on blast, but it's the truth. No one other than Charlie has the right to say it.

A few years after Charlie's dad visited her in Kansas, she had a dream involving her father. She dreamt he was at church with Desiree and Ruth. The setting was a church meeting, and in that meeting Rev. Reiss was in tears listening to horrible comments from parishioners who claimed to love him. Some of the comments and actions during the meeting were unbelievable. Rev. Reiss sat in the pulpit with his arms wrapped around himself, head lowered, while he wept in disbelief of what he heard.

Rev. Reiss exited the church. While walking down the driveway Ruth met him and put her arms around him in an attempt to comfort him. He walked ahead of Ruth, and in that moment, Charlie could see her dad, dressed immaculately as usual. Black suit, crisp white shirt matching tie, and buffed black dress shoes. He was known for his style. However, when she saw his face, it was skeletal. Rev. Reiss continued to walk and suddenly he was lifted up into a cloud, and went out of her sight. When he returned, his attire was changed. His suit was white as snow. He was calm and ready to proceed with whatever would come his way.

Charlie believes the dream was a message from the Lord. She, like her mother, knew the Lord communicated with them through the interpretation of dreams. However, Charlie had no idea the dream was clarification for upcoming events in the Reverends' life.

Wesley experience devastating blows from the church and its officials. They used his talent, made promises of promotion within the church. However, none of the promises were fulfilled. In the COGIC religion, the officials assign preacher to churches in need of a pastor. Wesley took many assignments, but never had success as a pastor. During the assignments, he worked construction jobs and used personal money to pay the churches utility bills amongst other financial obligations. One assignment stands out in her mind. Wesley was assigned to pastor a large church; however, the church member did not accept him as pastor. They were vocal in demonstrating their dislike of him. Wesley was deeply hurt and dismayed by their disdain of him. Ruth helped Wesley out of that church building. She actually showed affection toward her stepfather and told him he did not have to put up with that type treatment. Ruth said, "Come on, Daddy, let's get out of here."

When the meeting at the large church ended and the family discussed the situation, Charlie remembered her dream. She realized the Lord revealed what was going to happen to Rev. Reiss. It's amazing how some are gifted in communicating with the highest power, and the communication is confirmed as witnessed by others. Charlie claims it as one of the gifts of the spirit.

TRAVELING PREACHER

Wesley pursued his initial calling. He was called to be a traveling evangelist. He traveled preaching throughout the East and West Coast. Wesley was associated with some prominent preachers who invited him to run revivals. He loved running revivals by using a tent to contain the crowd and to attract those who wouldn't normally attend the church. Some of the revivals lasted thirty days. Those revivals were crusades like the ones ran by Billy Graham. During the revival days, many people gave their lives to Christ. Charlie was one of the converts during one of her father's last tent revivals. Charlie was getting baptized, but refused to let the pastors put her head under the water. Reason being if the spirit was high, they might get carried away and forget to let her up for air.

Charlie loved it when Wesley finished a revival and returned home. He would open his briefcase and allow her to collect all the change inside. Sometimes, she would collect upward of twenty dollars in coins.

Wesley was a great man and father to Charlie. He did the best he could to provide and to show affection to those who desired it. He loved children and could beat most at games played in those days. For example, jacks, jump rope, badminton, and shooting marbles was his specialty. Wesley was a great preacher, studied and learned from other men in the same craft. He had his own preaching style and convinced many that Jesus Christ was Lord and Savior. Wesley lost his battle with cancer spring of 1999. However, he lost the zest for life long before cancer crept in and suffocated him.

THE FUNERAL

In spring 1999, Rev. Reiss was in the hospital because of cancer. The doctors prepared the family and advised he may not recover. The Reverend was in the ICU, in grave condition as the cancer spread, introducing additional complications. During the next few days, Charlie worked during the day while remaining in contact with Desiree and the hospital staff for updates regarding her father's condition. After work, Charlie went to the hospital and spent the rest of the evening with her parents. The next day, she was up repeating the process.

However, after several days on a ventilator and seemingly at death's door, Rev. Reiss sat up in his hospital bed. To the doctor's and nurse's surprise, Rev. Reiss was fully conscious, asking about the NBA. He requested his glasses and a newspaper. Desiree contacted Charlie with the news, but she wasn't receptive to what she said. Charlie told Desiree, "Daddy is dying. Don't play around." Desiree assured Charlie that her information was accurate; she put Rev. Reiss on the phone so that Charlie could hear his voice. Immediately Charlie left work and arrived at the hospital straight away. She could not believe her eyes. Wesley watched basketball and reviewed the newspaper just as he had done before. It was a miracle. The Lord brought him back to his family. Some thought it would allow the Reverend and his family time for official goodbyes, as he was previously in a coma and unresponsive.

Eventually, the Reverend returned home to receive hospice care. The hospice staff was gracious and gently acknowledged that Wesley was alive; however, they explained he wouldn't survive. Charlie became aware that the medical explanation about her father's condition was based on science. Even though most didn't want to accept it, they must. Thank goodness for man's ability to research and study the human body. The study outcomes allow medical staff to help the family grieve while knowing why death is ultimately imminent. They were knowledgeable about the case and told the family almost down to the day and hour when the Reverend might die. And like clockwork, the day wasn't far off. Wesley took his final rest.

The family filled Desiree's apartment. Charlie, Lee, and their daughters, spouses, and grandchildren were there. When the funeral staff entered the apartment, they found Charlie sitting at her father's bedside. Charlie watched a miracle take place during a time of grief and sorrow. One had to capture the moment as God did his work. It was a terrifying and wonderful experience. The room was quiet as Rev. Reiss lay in his bed, unable to speak, but could see Charlie and hear her last words. She expressed how much she loved and cared for him and hated to see her father go.

Charlie felt satisfied; she'd done all in her power to help comfort him. She also prayed the Reverend could hear her words but understood his spirit was already with the Lord, as Charlie believed angels in the room created the time between herself and her father as he passed away. She watched him take his last breath, and the final heartbeat she heard from the monitor resting above his bed made a loud beep. Suddenly, Charlie was back to reality and knew it was over. The officials announced him deceased and stated the date and time for the record. The funeral staff escorted Rev. Reiss to his destination.

Charlie and Desiree needed to plan the funeral. However, Desiree wanted the situation to be about her and what her needs were. Desiree was always selfish, demanding most situations revolve around her. Desiree let Charlie finalize the funeral arrangements while she planned her wardrobe for the day. Once the church announced Rev. Reiss's passing, many donated condolence cards stuffed with money, which Desiree kept and spent on herself. She didn't seem outwardly upset or in anguish over the death, to the point Charlie questioned Desiree's demeanor. On occasion, Desiree exhibited so much emotion one would think her husband's death would warrant a similar display.

In an attempt to ready themselves for the funeral, Charlie and Desiree embarked on a shopping trip that Charlie would remember for years to come. Charlie nervously moved through the shopping mall, while Desiree seemed to enjoy the journey. She shopped for hours, sampling numerous outfits and shoes while ensuring matching purses and church hats were available for the choosing. Desiree had a saleslady at her beck and call. The saleslady took red, beige, floral, and other styled suits to Desiree's dressing room. The two of them had a casual conversation and seemed to enjoy themselves. The time seemed to stand still as Charlie sat in a chair, waiting for the shopping trip from hell to end. And it did. The cashier totaled suits, purses, hats, and shoes. My goodness, what a total for a two-day event. Oh well, Desiree would have choices if one outfit wasn't suitable. There were additional items to consider.

The ladies had a memorial service and an out-of-town funeral to attend. On the evening of the memorial, Charlie drove to Desiree's apartment to help her get dressed for the occasion. Charlie noticed Desiree hadn't opened the recently purchased items boxed up by the cashier. She was trying to understand which suit Desiree would wear. To Charlie's surprise, Desiree walked out into the living room wearing an old tattered dress. It wasn't clean or pressed. Charlie asked, "Is that what you are wearing to the memorial service?" With a quick turn of her head, Desiree looked at Charlie and said yes. Under the heaviness of her father's death and wanting the memorial to go well, she dropped the subject. At the out-of-town funeral, Desiree picked a second uninspired getup. Charlie couldn't believe Desiree would be inappropriately dressed, as people knew her for her impeccable taste in fashion.

This ensemble was from the back of her closet, something she hadn't worn in recent years. It just didn't fit the occasion. Charlie was upset based on the shopping trip; numerous complete outfits were purchased but not worn to either service. It was baffling. How could she disrespect the Reverend and not represent the family in her typical classy way? Charlie always wondered how Desiree could pull a stunt like that at such a critical time. After all, people knew Rev. Reiss and Desiree in COGIC for dressing well. In past years some paused to see what they would wear to different church affairs and then verbally state how wonderful and impeccably dressed they were.

The out-of-town trip was nerve-racking as Charlie and her daughters along with Desiree returned home. During the journey home, Desiree complained of being sick and nauseous, and she requested to stop the car seemingly every ten miles or so. No one knew how to handle the situation, as Desiree was uncontrollable. And looking into her eyes, Charlie realized Desiree had no clue what she was doing or saying. It was the trip from hell that couldn't end soon enough. Desiree's behavior was weird and off-kilter. And Charlie knew her mother required help. Charlie could not control or solve what Desiree was experiencing.

THE CAREGIVER

After returning home and settling in and attempting to calm herself, Charlie consulted a doctor about Desiree's actions. She questioned how Desiree reacted to the Reverend's death, along with the shopping trip and how she acted during the journey home. After speaking with Charlie and evaluating her responses to Desiree's questions, the doctor indicated if Charlie didn't get Desiree under medical care immediately, she could be held accountable for senior abuse. The doctor's comments were puzzling, as Charlie wasn't aware of what the doctor was saying. She asked, to be clear, "Exactly what are you saying about Desiree? Why does she need immediate medical care?"

The doctor explained that Desiree was in the early stages of dementia that could eventually develop into Alzheimer's disease. The doctor set up office visits so she could examine Desiree and give an official diagnosis. Desiree visited the doctor several times, and during each visit, her attitude and demeanor were more sporadic. The doctor helped Charlie understand what was happening and what role she played in the situation. "As Desiree's daughter and next of kin," the doctor told Charlie, "you are responsible for her welfare." Charlie took the news to heart as she did in most circumstances and immediately researched the meaning of *dementia*. She also talked with several other adults who were caregivers and experienced similar situations with their parents.

The doctor further explained that dementia is a vast medical condition that affects brain function. It's a disorder of mental capacity overshadowed by memory loss, personality changes, and impaired reasoning. There are numerous systems of dementia, which cause difficulty in diagnosis.

Some define *dementia* as an umbrella term for conditions involving cognitive functioning. Dementia is not a normal part of aging. As we age, most experience memory loss. However, dementia causes severe impairments, disrupting daily life.

The doctor suggested a facility that offered services Desiree required. Charlie knew her mother had to be cared for but didn't want to place her in a nursing facility. However, Charlie contacted the facility suggested by the doctor. The director of the facility met with Charlie and explained that most residents' life expectancy would likely be limited. Mostly, men, they tend to die sometimes within sixty to ninety days from admittance.

It wasn't long after meeting the director that Charlie received notification that there was room for her mother. To get Desiree situated in the facility, Charlie had a few things to take care of. The Medicare personnel interviewed Charlie and Desiree to determine if the facility offered what Desiree required. They sent Desiree to numerous doctors, who performed evaluations to confirm the original doctor's diagnosis. After the assessments, the last thing Charlie needed was to hear Desiree saying "I need to get help." Desiree had diabetes and needed assistance with dietary and medication schedules. She also required assistance with daily hygiene and personal care. In other words, Desiree could no longer care for herself.

One incident was memorable. Charlie remembered Desiree imagining someone was breaking into her apartment through the glass sliding doors of her patio. She stated, three white men were in her apartment, and she fought them off. Somehow Desiree managed to call 911; they, in turn, called Charlie to let her know Mom was in trouble. Charlie wasn't sure how the 911 operator knew to contact her or obtained her cellphone number. However, she was grateful they contacted her. The medical attendants and police arrived, and Desiree's blood sugar was down to 45 (70–100 is average). She was disoriented and continued speaking about the men breaking into her home. At this point, she could have gone into a diabetic coma. The attendant administered a glucose injection into Desiree's right thigh. Once she regained consciousness, Desiree admitted she needed help.

Charlie immediately sprang into action, getting her mother's apartment closed up and placing her belongings in storage. Charlie was the next of kin but was alone in making important decisions for and about her mother. She had siblings, but they chose not to engage other than to say what they would or wouldn't do if it was up to them. Ultimately her brother said, "Charlie, you are with her, and it's your decision. You know what she needs." Charlie was left to make the arrangements for Desiree while dealing with the emotional pull of grief, getting to know the staff at the facility, and most of all, learning to balance visits to the facility, work, and home life.

Desiree, like other residents in the facility, found it difficult to adjust to the new environment. Eventually, she became familiar with her new home and the other residents. Charlie witnessed a definite change in Desiree. Somehow, she wasn't Mama anymore. At times, Desiree didn't recognize Charlie as her daughter. Charlie and her mother were relatively close as the mother-daughter relationship goes. The facility transported Desiree to church on first Sundays. Charlie met her there, and they would enter the church together. On one of those occasions, Charlie noticed the change in her mother's eyes. Her eyes didn't focus on any one thing; she looked past Charlie while speaking to her as if she were a stranger. Then she returned to reality, saying, "Girl, I didn't know that was you." That statement devasted Charlie.

As time progressed, it was difficult relating to Desiree and problematic for the nursing staff to assist. She demanded that everyone respect her as she acted out and was rude and hateful toward the nursing staff. Charlie received numerous phone calls from the nursing director, explaining how Desiree's interactions with the team were disruptive and how she treated them as they attempted to administer their duties in assisting residents with day-to-day functions. Desiree always had a problem with the food. And sometimes would not eat because the food looked weird or wasn't to her taste. Desiree was disagreeable and had no qualms letting others know her thoughts. It was almost like having a child in daycare or school and receiving a phone call from the principal about your child misbehaving. Charlie realized Desiree heightened her defenses because she could no longer care for herself. Defying the nurses was Desiree's attempt at being independent and still in charge of her own life.

Some may have the wrong impression. Maybe Charlie thought too highly of herself or believed she always performed adequately. She was human and subject to error. Her judgment of Desiree was not malicious or meant to defame her character. Charlie expressed her thoughts about her mother and wanted others to know it's okay to speak your mind. She internalized feelings on many occasions and should have spoken up before now. Charlie spent most of her life as a mediator, the police and peacemaker within her family. When problems arose, Charlie was the person the family confided in. Why she took on that persona was the ultimate question. She honored her parents, right or wrong. She listened to her siblings complain about their parents and how they were raised and how their parents disappointed them during childhood.

Charlie took on the heavy load of doling out money as if she and Lee had it in abundance. She always gave too much. And wanted to satisfy every request; Charlie used her credit rating to obtain an apartment for a relative. She also loaned nine hundred dollars to the same relative; the relative never paid the money back or mentioned it to Charlie or Lee again. The relative lived in the apartment for almost thirty days then moved out just as the rent was due. Charlie wanted to make amends for their parents' way of life and how her siblings felt about the past. She knew it wasn't her responsibility, but she felt obligated and wedged between her parents and siblings.

Charlie met herself coming and going as she continued to comfort and care for her mother as she had always done. One evening, a nurse told Charlie, "We will take care of your mother. No need for you to run errands or pick up medication from the pharmacy anymore. Relax, she is in good hands." And she was. The developing stage of dementia and Desiree's natural ability to be disagreeable were more evident than before. As time progressed, an unrecognizable personality emerged. Desiree was now a different person.

Even though the facility director advised that some residents may not live long in the environment, Desiree lived there for many years. She called it home. Sometimes during outings with family,

Desiree would say "I'm ready to go home." Desiree was speaking of the nursing facility; she was comfortable there. Charlie and other family members experienced different scenarios while visiting Desiree at the facility. Some were comical, but other events frightened some, and at times, Charlie was speechless in the moments of Desiree's anguish.

THE FOUNDATION

The Reiss family's foundation was the Church of God in Christ, sometimes referred to as the COGIC church. It is the largest Pentecostal denomination in the United States. Charlie was born into the religion, as her mother and others in the lineage. Bishop C. H. Mason started the belief in 1895, approximately thirty years after the Emancipation Proclamation. Bishop Mason's parents were slaves who lived and worked on a farm near Memphis, Tennessee. They attended the same church as their owners, the Missionary Baptist Church. The Bishop was baptized and ordained as a teenager in that church. However, the church expelled him for preaching a new doctrine of sanctification and holiness.

After slavery, the Bishop and others were free to worship as they pleased. The doctrine of sanctification and holiness is the emphasis of the religion. The origin came to Bishop Mason in a vision. And it was derived from events that transpired on Pentecost as described in Acts of the Apostles. Bishop Mason combined his vision with the events from Pentecost's day and delivered the message to his followers.

On the day of Pentecost, there was an outpouring of supernatural manifestation that overcame everyone in the upper room. The visitation outcome revealed the gifts of the spirit, which Jesus promised to those who waited on the anointing. The Father, Son, and the Holy Ghost empowered the believers with the spirit's gifts, as described in scripture. Some may refer to them as the Trinity, all of whom are required to keep one saved while living on the earth. After death, the greatest gift of salvation is that man will stand before God with Jesus at his right hand in all his glory. Yes, there is the judgment, and after that, those who believed and confessed that Jesus Christ is the Savior of the world will have eternal life.

While attending a revival in Los Angeles, California, Bishop Mason was eager to feel what others displayed. The Bishop describes his experience with salvation in a dramatic way: "I felt flames in my mouth that went through my body. I spoke in tongues almost immediately. I could not speak in English. I only spoke in unknown tongues." The Bishop's testimony inspired others to seek the same anointing.

Notwithstanding the doctrine and revelations from the Holy Spirit, some were obsessed with adding to the list of sins that could lead to one's detriment. When Charlie was growing up in the church, the pastors preached fire and brimstone. No one was joyful or excited by the preached word because of the delivery. In those days, most preachers were self-proclaimed, uneducated, and only associated with others of the same mindset.

The pastors believed those of other religions were sinners because some drank liquor, smoked cigarettes, and may have played pool or a card game on occasion. It seems like someone took 2nd Corinthians 6:17 literally. The scripture was about being unequally yoked and worshiping idol gods, not about separating from the world in its entirety. "We are in the world, but not of it" describes the characteristics of a Christian. One should strive to live a life pleasing to God while existing on earth.

The characteristics of COGIC encompass a gamut of sins. There are too many to list in this writing. Those familiar with COGIC are well aware of the sins that lead straight to hell. Charlie was afraid during most sermons—it seemed as if everyone was going to hell. The humorous part is, some of the COGIC leadership imbibed but did so secretly. Charlie remembers overhearing her father describe one of the high-ranking bishops who wanted Rev. Reiss to purchase liquor for him. The Bishop couldn't physically go into the liquor store, so he assigned others to do his dirty work.

Charlie couldn't believe what she heard or that the presiding Bishop was a recovering acholic who relapsed or backslid, as said in the church. People knew of other indiscretions, and no one lost their positions in the church. In COGIC, there are numerous rules, human-made sins, and unspoken requirements one must abide by to demonstrate devotion to the church and the congregation. The message received from the apparent displays influences some to believe perfection is required for salvation and to be Holy Ghost filled. Charlie's grandmother Flo was an example of someone who wanted to be perfect.

In keeping with the leadership of COGIC, Charlie wasn't acquainted with some family members because they were Baptist or Methodist and believed to be unsaved. Family reunions, funerals, and other situations that could lead to Charlie associating with family and friends outside the COGIC church were off-limits. However, Charlie attended the public school with three of her cousins. They recognized Charlie's last name and knew her father was a preacher and where they lived. Charlie was thrilled to know her cousins; they attended the same schools from primary through high school. Charlie developed friendships with her cousins but kept the relationships hidden from her parents.

Although Charlie grew up in the COGIC church, she was concerned she may not be saved. Charlie didn't dance in church like the others or feel the Holy Spirit's utterance, who some say prompted them to speak in tongues. She knew Jesus and believed in him. However, she didn't comprehend the actions of some in the congregation. During some church services, when the spirit of the Lord was high, the choir sang their hearts out, and the music was at its highest level. People ran around the walls of the church, others cried tears of joy, and many exhibited a quickening of the Holy Spirit.

Their bodies flailed about, arms outreached as if touching the hem of His garment, and some people passed out under the anointing of the Holy Spirit. Desiree was one who openly expressed her salvation through dancing, singing, and speaking in tongues almost every church service. Charlie didn't feel the power of the Holy Spirit until later in life. She knew the spiritual touch is real and praised God for allowing her to experience His presence.

Some are baffled about living a saved life and existing in the world. On Sundays, the congregation seemed happy and excited in anticipation of dancing across the church's dusty wooden floors. Some wanted to show off their church hats, and others were spectators. They all but took bets on who would be the first to engage in the holy dance. However, come Monday, the environment was different. People seemed distant, as if they were disappointed Sunday was over. That's when the arguing started in the Reiss home. Inevitably, there would be an issue to resolve from the previous week or years past. Cursing, slamming doors, and rushing out of the front door were the events of the day.

Charlie wished she could understand why her parents were different at home as opposed to Sundays at church. They professed to be saved and filled with the Holy Spirit. Her father was a preacher; her mother was the church musician and a missionary. However, home life didn't represent or equal the joy displayed on Sunday mornings. Charlie thought that being saved doesn't change the person but allows one to experience a personal relationship with Jesus Christ. It's an experience, an ongoing phase. We know God cannot tolerate sin; that's why he sent his only begotten son Jesus Christ as the go-between to forgive our sins and show us faultless before God. Thank God for his mercy and his son Jesus Christ.

Some may misconstrue salvation with living in a utopia; however, we must exist in this world. No one is instantly changed or a different person with a prayer or exclaiming their belief in Jesus Christ; it is a work in progress. However, we should be kind and treat others well. That includes the significant other, and that's the piece of the pie that was missing in Rev. Reiss and Desiree's marriage. They started their relationship under the guise of being in love but didn't develop a friendship in the interim.

Rev. Reiss attempted to retrain Desiree because Flo failed as a mother when Desiree was a child. And Desiree, seemingly unaware of her place in the world she created when she married Rev. Reiss, didn't make life any easier. Desiree didn't have anyone to model the behaviors she lacked. Her mother was presumably married; however, she didn't focus on family life. Her entire existence was about the church. Therefore, Desiree was confused about her role in life.

Society is more aware of how one should conduct themselves these days. There are many self-help books available that outline how we move globally regardless of our positions in life. Anything we need to know is available on the internet. If you are the first lady of the church or even the pastor, there are existing guidelines to assist in a prosperous lifestyle. In previous years self-proclaimed church leaders shot from the hip. Most were unable to read and depended on someone in the congregation to read scripture.

When the reader finished, the preacher would expound on that scripture. However, the sermons did not inspire most. Not sure how the congregation came to the point of connecting the sermon to life experiences. But the church would eventually go into praise and worship following the sermon.

Nowadays, people are educated and have studied the scriptures for themselves. They don't depend on someone else to explain how salvation works. The clergy attend seminary and pride themselves in explaining the scriptures and relating scripture to one's lifestyles. I guess once you know better, you do better.

CHURCH ADVENTURES

One Sunday morning, Carlton Pearson was in the audience at church. He attended Oral Robert University and came to Charlie's church to fellowship. The junior choir was on the program to perform two selections during church service that day. However, when Carlton Pearson was invited to the pulpit to have a few words, he requested the junior choir sing a song with him. Carlton brought his organist named David along. Once David reset the organ and began to play, church service was epic.

Carlton wasn't much older than Charlie; he was handsome and a college student. His presence increased the chances that some would follow in his footsteps and pursue a college education. Carlton was saved and knew how to get others involved in praise and worship. Everyone was impressed with Carlton and wished he would become a member of the church. After all, having someone of his caliber in their church could influence other young people to seek a more spiritual lifestyle. With Charlie's father being a preacher, she had the opportunity to meet Carlton. He and Rev. Reiss became friends; he ate dinner at Charlie's house. She couldn't tell anyone about her attraction to Carlton, so she admired him from afar.

After experiencing Carlton's method of praise and worship, Charlie became interested in the music department. After all, her mother was a church musician. Charlie had access to the church instruments; however, if the pastor nicknamed Preacher was in the building, she couldn't play either instrument until he left the premises. He'd say, "No banging on that," meaning the church instruments. Once he left the church, Desiree and Charlie played the music together. Desiree was an accomplished musician; she humored Charlie by allowing her to play along. Desiree owned the popular gospel albums from artists such as James Cleveland and the Hawkins Singers. Charlie could play the music just by listening and echoing what she heard.

Once again, Rev. Reiss was assigned to pastor a small church in one of those rural areas mentioned earlier. Charlie had a situation one day at the church; she was supposed to perform a solo before her father preached. She started to sing and began playing the piano; her voice sounded off; she was in the wrong key. Charlie was embarrassed and immediately returned to her seat in the audience; she never attempted a solo again. Her parents encouraged the musical endeavor and allowed Charlie to play the piano at home. She could play but suffered stage fright. Desiree told Charlie, "You should've started the song over again. Don't let that stop you."

Charlie continued with the music at church; her father pastored numerous churches, and most didn't have a musician. No one expected a professional, and they accepted Charlie's talents. Desiree was in charge of the musical part of the service, and Charlie was her backup. The city had many small churches located in rural areas. Charlie traveled with her parents, as Rev. Reiss preached; Desiree and Charlie supplied the music.

One of the church services was in Kansas. The family visited the city zoo and enjoyed the day. However, they purchased a soda from a vending machine. Charlie consumed the soda; she became ill. She felt drugged, lightheaded, and probably should've gone to the hospital. Her parents watched her and didn't let her sleep. Charlie was in bed for the rest of the day; eventually, the bad feeling subsided. Her parents let her stay home from church. They probably felt guilty; after all, her father purchased the soda that caused Charlie's illness. Charlie told her father, "Daddy, it's okay."

Rev. Reiss organized a church of his own. The services were in an old abandoned movie theater. The surrounding area was suspect; there was a bar across the street, and the ladies of the night graced the roads at will. The building was so large that it would never be filled with church people unless there was a funeral. Again, Desiree was on piano, and Charlie was on the organ. The family singing group performed their memorable songs. However, the family was the only people in attendance. Some of Charlie's friends attended the church for a time but eventually left.

Charlie's parents continued their endeavor with church growth. They held the regular church services and invited others to attend. The congregation was small, consisting of a handful of members. It was Sunday evening; time for church. The evening service was YPWW, which is an acronym for "Young people, willing workers." Desiree pretended to be sick and told her husband she was staying home.

For some reason, Charlie assumed if she washed her hair, there was no way her father would make her attend church tonight. After all, Desiree wasn't going, so Charlie thought she was in the clear. Rev. Reiss bellowed down the hall, "It's time to go," aiming his voice toward Charlie's bedroom door. She opened the door and pointed to her hair. Her father said, "Let's go." His voice was stern and sounded like Charlie wasn't getting her way this time. Long story short, Charlie attended YPWW with half of her hair pressed, and the other half was nappy.

THE EVANGELIST

The church started by Rev. Reiss didn't last. He returned to working with the presiding bishop to obtain assignments for outlying churches. His dreams of becoming a pastor of a vibrant church never materialized. Charlie believed Rev. Reiss was an evangelist, not a pastor. There is a difference. A pastor is a spiritual overseer; an evangelist or evangelism is winning or reviving personal commitments to Christ. Rev. Reiss was an evangelist. Charlie wasn't sure why her father wanted to be a pastor or bishop. He knew his calling and traveled extensively in the capacity of an evangelist.

Charlie remembered his travels and how Desiree joined him on some of the excursions. Rev. Reiss received an invitation from one of their former pastors to come and run a revival, with expenses paid. Her parents traveled to California to run a thirty-day revival. The invitation was a blessing, financially and emotionally, for Rev. Reiss. Charlie's parents left for California in the family car. It was a white Cadillac with red interior. This car was her father's pride and joy. Her father always liked and drove nice cars. He was proud to own a Cadillac, and representing his family in grand style made him proud.

The trip was going well until they reached Arizona. They stopped for gas. Rev. Reiss went into the service station to pay for gas, and when he returned to the car, it was smoking. Black and blue smoke billowed from beneath the vehicle. He yelled and told Desiree, "GET OUT OF THE CAR!" She didn't realize what was happening but got out anyway. Desiree joined her husband on the side of the road.

The car burned from the back bumper to the front bumper and back again. The vehicle was in flames; in the interim, the fire department arrived. They checked on Charlie's parents to make sure they were okay. The fire department told them, "The car is a total loss, including your possessions." Charlie imagined her father expressed his dismay with the comment "My god" while shaking his head in disbelief. After gathering his thoughts, Rev. Reiss called the pastor in California with the unfortunate news. There was no internet, Skype, or email, so finding transportation into Los Angeles wouldn't be easy. They waited for hours in the hot Arizona sun before being rescued.

They finally reached California. The pastor was gracious and honored Rev. Reiss and Desiree in a manner they hadn't witnessed before. Rev. Reiss replaced everything lost in the fire through the outpouring of gifts from church members coupled with the money from the revival. However, Charlie was in Tulsa. There was minimal communication between Charlie and her parents. Telephones were scarce, and long-distance calls were expensive.

Initially, Charlie was supposed to stay with a distant cousin of Desiree's. They were members of the same church and agreed to take care of Charlie while her parents were out-of-town. The cousin lived near Charlie's school, so she walked to school from there. Charlie returned to the cousin's home and concluded she wasn't welcome after hearing a discussion between the cousin and her grown daughter.

Desiree's cousin pretended to like Charlie, but it was apparent she didn't like her. So Charlie left the cousin's house to find her brother. Iverson left home and lived with his best friend. Charlie found the place and let Iverson know the situation. He took her in and made sure she was clean and fed. He was a good brother who always looked out for her. Charlie attended school and stopped by the family home to change clothes and listen to rhythm and blues since Rev. Reiss wasn't home. Rev. Reiss and Desiree were in Los Angeles for three months. During that time, Charlie was on her own. She was a latchkey kid; Charlie knew how to take care of herself. However, she needed her parents like most children.

REMEMBERING
SUBURBIA

When they returned to Tulsa, Charlie ran to the door to greet her parents. Before she knew it, the family moved out of Liz's house into their own home. It was a lovely house in a relatively new neighborhood. The Reiss family were the first black people to move onto that street. One by one, their white neighbors moved out. It was significant, as integration was on the horizon; this was a preview of what Charlie would face when she began high school in the fall. When the school opened, the environment was strange. It was her first time being around white people, and the situation was the same for the teachers and the white students.

The public school system enforced the integration law in her town. It would be a new world Charlie had to navigate through. She developed her method of recognizing teachers and students by the hair and eye color. Soon she knew who she was speaking to and whether integration would be a stumbling block or a higher education method. The school was new on the north side of town; Charlie's class would be the first seniors to graduate from the school. She had to survive three years at the new school while managing her grades, friendships, and personal life.

Charlie was about to enroll in the new high school. She stood at the front desk of the school with Wesley to fill out the school forms. She asked Wesley if she could attend the only black high school in town. Charlie wanted to be part of the Hornets marching band. They sounded great and looked even better in their unique band uniforms. However, the school had a reputation for causing disturbances during football outings. Some people fought during some of the games. Some think the fights were to intimidate the visiting schools and their supporters. Charlie didn't care about their reputation; she wanted to be part of the Hornets marching band. She went to the new school as planned. When plans changed or things didn't go her way; Charlie would pacify herself by observing the weather or thinking about the next fresh hamburger from the Lot-A-Burger stand. This time she focused on the weather; after all, it was her favorite time of the year.

The winter session ended quickly. Charlie survived and was looking forward to springtime. However, the happy thoughts were short-lived. A new school emblem was freshly installed. The symbol was on the floor near the front doors of the school. Some people thought they should walk around the logo, and others considered it part of the walkway. It didn't take long for a fight to break out. When the bell rang and school was over, a young black student stepped on the emblem, attempting to leave the building. He was confronted by a large white boy who screamed, "HEY, DON'T WALK ON THAT!" The black student continued to move forward and tried to open the school door, but he was pulled back into the building. A fight ensued. Soon, there was a race riot.

The police came to the school. People ran through the building, seeking a way out. Charlie called Desiree and told her about the riot. Desiree told Charlie, "Come home now." Charlie was afraid to leave the building because she was alone. Desiree didn't drive, so Charlie had to walk home. While walking to her house, a car approached. Five white boys were in the car. As the vehicle passed Charlie, someone in the car threw an object at her. Charlie was stunned in her tracks. She saw stars and had difficulty breathing. Once Charlie was able to compose herself, she realized what happened. The boys threw a wad of paper at her. She picked up the bundle of paper and took it home to show her parents.

The wad of paper was thick and folded in the shape of a star. It was hard to the touch and was aimed directly at Charlie; they hit her in the throat. Charlie's father thought it could have put her eye out or caused more physical harm. Thank God, the boys kept moving in the opposite direction. However, they knew Charlie was hurt. The boys looked back at her and laughed as she choked and cried for help. Charlie stayed home for a few days to recuperate. From that point, her father drove her to and from school.

There was one hiccup when it came to Wesley taking Charlie to and from school. It was her hairstyle. She wore an afro, but her father disapproved. He thought an afro was a militant act showing defiance to the authorities. After all, he was a preacher and well-known in the community. For his daughter to style her hair like Angela Davis or Stokely Carmichael was wrong and unacceptable. The Black Power and Civil Rights movement influenced Charlie's style. However, COGIC did not engage in political activities. Most in Charlie's community didn't vote. They were neutral about most things outside of the church.

To keep her hairdo concealed, Charlie braided her hair and wore a headscarf when riding with Wesley. He worked the early shift, so Charlie arrived at school early enough to take her braids down and fluff out her afro. Long story short, this was Charlie's routine until she could no longer keep the lie going. She was not a good liar and felt guilty for keeping the secret from her father. They were good friends and had a great relationship. So to lie to him wasn't fair. Charlie decided to tell her parents about her hairdo and the jeans she wore at school without their permission. Yes, she covered up two lies; she tried to fit in with the rest of the students. However, the family's religion stipulated what the members should wear, and the list didn't include pants or jeans.

The discussion continued late into the night. Charlie stood her ground and advocated for herself without disrespecting her parents. Desiree didn't care but sided with Wesley to show a united facade. Finally, her parents relented. However, there was one stipulation from Wesley: "No afros or jeans when attending church." Charlie was relieved and happy with the decision. She could relax and dress in the current style like her peers. The school systems lifted the conservative dress codes. Girls could wear jeans or pants to school. Therefore, the school system supported the idea and helped Charlie get her point across to her parents.

Charlie and her best friend met at church. Her name was Carrol. She moved to Charlie's town from Memphis, Tennessee, and she was a relative of Desiree's missionary friends. The girls met and immediately became friends. Charlie was standing on the steps of the church, Carrol and one of her brothers approached. Charlie introduced herself; she knew Carrol was new to the city and the church. She invited Carrol to come and sit in the youth section of the church. The girls passed notes to each other during church service. It turns out that the girls were assigned to attend the same high school. They planned to meet each other at school the next day.

On the first day of the tenth grade, the girls met under the school campus flagpole. They were in the minority as the only two black girls joining the marching band as their homeroom class. The band instructor was a Native American. He didn't understand black people, and black people couldn't comprehend why he was prejudiced against another minority. Charlie concluded that discrimination was just a misunderstanding about different cultures. However, the discovery wasn't why either girl attended school. They were in school to learn, but they would face some stumbling blocks to either help them mature or tear down their self-esteem.

The following brings this reading full circle. The girls were together when the riot began. Carrol rode the bus to school, and to avoid missing the bus home, she had to leave Charlie on her own. Carrol had no idea that fellow students would attack Charlie because of her skin color. Charlie's parents called the school and spoke with a school counselor. They reported the incident, but Charlie could not identify any of those involved.

There were other situations involving teachers who had to teach black students. They had no qualms sharing their distain about the new requirement. One of the office machines teachers didn't think black students could grasp the concept of her class. She didn't believe they were smart enough to learn the process. Charlie was one of the students who wanted to succeed in the course. Her grade was below a B average. Charlie asked the teacher for help and what she could do to raise her grade point. The teacher told her, "You'll never learn to use these machines." Naturally, Charlie was offended by the statement. She discussed the grade with Wesley, who decided to meet with the teacher to discuss the situation. During the meeting, the teacher could not make eye contact with Wesley. She had very little to say about Charlie or her grades. Wesley repeated what the teacher told Charlie. The teacher offered a feeble explanation, denying her previous statement. It was clear that this lady had no intention of teaching or getting to know any black students. To avoid receiving a failing grade, Charlie transferred to a different office machines class.

She didn't hold a grudge but never forgot how the previous teacher treated her. Sometimes, it takes an insult to push one to achieve. Charlie was successful in office administration. It was the vocation the first office machines teacher prophesied Charlie would never succeed in. Charlie worked in the field for over twenty-five years. She refers to a quote by Maya Angelou, which states, "I've learned that people will forget what you said, people will forget what you did, but people will never forget how you made them feel." The quote was relevant then, as it is now. Carrol, Charlie's best friend, experienced prejudice as well. She soldiered through and became a schoolteacher and counselor. She earned many accolades and retired from public school after forty years of service.

During the integration period, students in other parts of the state had to integrate. One student who was a star football player in his current school and held a B+ grade point average had to change schools. The new school was thirty miles from his neighborhood, so the students were taken to the new facility by bus. Upon entering the school and meeting the football coach, the football player felt awful leaving familiar surroundings to attend school. The coach told him, "You can't be a starter on this football team. You are a freshman. You can dress out, but you can't play."

The student became cynical and lost his zeal for school and football. By the second semester, he quit football and came to school for attendance only. A former teacher who happened to be black was instrumental in helping his former students achieve excellence in the new school. The football player took the advice of his former teacher. He became an engineer and had a successful career in the oil industry. Charlie concluded, "The actions of others can't limit one's destiny. It's up to the individual to succeed in life. One can either buckle under the pressure of ignorance or choose to believe in themselves."

The school bell rang; it was time for class to begin. The band was warming up on their instruments, and someone started playing the bass line from a song by Archie Bell called "Tighten Up." The band director wanted everyone to settle down and come to order. However, the music didn't stop; the band continued to play. The director was furious and yelled, "You people be quiet." He repeated the statement until everyone in the room was quiet. The band was silent because they were insulted because of the racist comment from the instructor.

Addressing the class as *you people* didn't go over well in a classroom filled with black students. Charlie left class and went to the front desk of the school and called her parents. She explained the situation to her parents; they visited the school that day. Wesley and Desiree talked with the assistant principal, who pretended he was interested in Charlie's protest. Even though it was only two words that offended the students, they were offensive. However, Charlie was the only student who expressed her discontentment.

Charlie graduated from high school. It was finally over; she could be an adult and make her own choices. She didn't graduate with honors or a college scholarship. Instead, she enrolled in Job Corps. In the interim, Charlie obtained a job at a steel company. They manufactured windows and doorframes for mobile homes. She worked there for three months while waiting for an opening at Job Corps. One day, there was a storm forecast to hit the city by late afternoon. The report was unbelievable because the weather had been beautiful the entire day. However, later that afternoon, the storm came over the city. They called it black ice because the ice formed on the streets, but it couldn't be seen by those traveling the roads. Charlie left the job early because of the storm. While driving home, she stayed close to the outside lanes and traveled at a low speed in case she hit an ice patch.

Charlie focused on driving while listening to the local gospel station. She thought the gospel music would calm her nerves. Before she knew it, she hit an ice patch. The ice was between two sloping pieces of land where pavement was laid, with deep ditches on either side of the road. When the car hit the ice, it immediately started spinning. The vehicle turned in a counterclockwise motion. It didn't travel forward but stayed in a circular motion until the gas tank was empty. Charlie held the steering wheel and took her foot off the gas. She didn't know what was about to happen but realized her life was flashing in front of her; she thought she would die. Charlie released the steering wheel, lifted her hands toward the heavens, and said, "Lord, I'm not ready yet." That's when she knew God saved her. She used all of her strength to open the driver's side door. Somehow, she stepped out of the car without being knocked down by the force of the spinning vehicle.

The strength was the power of the Lord; he made it possible for Charlie to exit the car. In her mind, this was a miraculous situation. She seemed to float out of the car, and when her feet touched the ground, she was back to herself. She remembered one of her favorite verses from Philippians 4:13, "I can do all things through Christ who strengthens me." Charlie didn't know it, but a crowd of people formed near her car. They wanted to help but couldn't. When she exited the vehicle, a man asked, "Are you okay, lady? You could've gotten killed getting out of the car like that." Charlie was shaking and nervous because of the event. After calming herself, she eventually drove home. When Charlie arrived at Wesley's, she stopped directly in front of the house and told him, "Daddy, get your car." It was a few weeks before she would drive again.

AND AWAY WE GO

Charlie arrived at Job Corps a few weeks later. She was excited about her new adventure, and she was ready to learn a skill. One of her classes involved training to be a rail caller for the railroad. She would be responsible for making sure trains were traveling on the right track. Charlie did well and received a job offer. However, the job was in Clovis, New Mexico, thousands of miles from her parents. Charlie told her parents about the job and the date of the interview. She traveled with the railroad representative to Clovis, New Mexico.

While traveling with the representative, people stared and whispered about the odd couple in the restaurant. They saw Charlie and the representative; they road in the car together and ate inside restaurants during the trip. It was too much for some. Blacks and whites didn't travel together in those days. However, the interview went well. All she needed to do was move to New Mexico to start her new career.

When Charlie returned from New Mexico, she went home to tell her parents about her travels. She was excited to tell them about her new job. However, immediately, when she stepped into the house, she knew something was about to bring her back to reality. Wesley cried and told Charlie, "I can't let you move to New Mexico." Charlie couldn't believe her ears. After all, she traveled thousands of miles in a car with a white man; she got the job. Why didn't he express his feeling earlier?

Charlie was taken aback but had to move forward with her life. She could no longer live in Wesley's house; she was ready to live her own life. Charlie had to turn the job down and explain why she could not accept the position to the railroad representative. Once the embarrassment subsided, Charlie decided college would be her

78

next stop. She packed her belongings, quit Job Corps, and enrolled in college. If she'd moved to New Mexico instead of going to college, she would've met Lee. He became the love of her life.

CHARLIE

Charlie received her acceptance letter from the university. She needed her parents to sign the loan papers because she was a minor and did not have a job. The Reiss family traveled to the university, which was an hour's drive from home. When they reached the campus, the receptionist directed them to the financial aid office.

When Wesley signed the paperwork, and the financial advisor settled the school expenditures, the financial advisor handed him a check. Remember, the electronic world did not exist; business took place in person via hard copy. So receiving a hard copy check was the norm.

The leftover money was for Charlie's living expenses. However, Wesley used some cash to purchase tires for his car and other personal items. He bought what he wanted with no explanation. There was an unspoken rule in the Reiss household that Charlie abided by: a child never challenges their parents. She was upset, but as usual, she kept quiet.

Charlie could not wait to leave Wesley and Desiree behind while pursuing her college career. Charlie and her best friend attended the same college, and they were roommates for the first semester. When the ladies arrived at the student union building to get their ID pictures taken, a young man was behind the camera. This guy did not say much but smiled and motioned to the ladies where to stand so he could snap their pictures.

Charlie became acquainted with other students on campus, and they invited her to a party later that night. Of course, Charlie attended the party, and that is where she met Lee. He took pictures of Charlie and her best friend earlier that day. However, Charlie would not become aware that Lee kept a separate photo of her for himself until later.

During the party, Charlie noticed a tall, handsome, quiet guy standing near the door. She told her best friend, "I am going to talk to him if it is the last thing I do." Most people smoked cigarettes during those days. So she pretended to need to light her cigarette. Charlie asked him, "Do you have a light?"

Lee struck a match for Charlie and green-lit their long-term relationship. It turned out that Lee was the smiling guy behind the camera. It seemed simple enough; however, their relationship moved quickly. Charlie and Lee were serious about each other and talked about getting married. However, neither family met their significant other.

It would be difficult for Wesley to accept any man who was romantically interested in Charlie. Furthermore, Lee's mother did not want him to marry anyone. Mostly because of her financial situation, she could not participate in the festivities. It turned out Charlie's family was as poor as Lee's mom. However, Wesley was a preacher and received monetary gifts from church members and Charlie's godmothers. He sustained his family from seasonal construction jobs. So paying for a wedding was doable, but Lee's mom wanted to contribute.

Charlie and Lee dated for nine months while planning their wedding, which took place during the summer of Lee's junior year at the university.

LEE AND CHARLIE

Lee and Charlie were married by the fall semester and needed a place to live. The university did not offer married housing on campus, so they obtained housing in the Indian Nations Apartment complex. It was a small one-bedroom apartment. They were so proud to acquire the apartment on their own; it was their first home together. The apartment complex's name may seem questionable, but it was acceptable to label objects, buildings, and sports teams according to the surrounding area during those days. The university was located in the middle of American Indian territory, hence the name "Indian Nations."

Von and Will were from Layton, Oklahoma, and they lived in the same apartment complex. Will played football, and Von was a home economics major. They lived two doors down from Charlie and Lee. The couples became friends. Moreover, Von attempted to teach Charlie how to cook and showed her a little sewing along the way. Von was talented in tailoring. She made a suit for her husband. Will was proud to wear a suit fashioned by his new wife.

People gathered in the student union daily to play spades. Sometimes, the line was four to five people waiting for a chance to play. Will and Lee played cards. Furthermore, if a person did not know how to play exceptionally well and talk aggressively to and about others attempting to play, everyone's time would be wasted. Some people skipped classes, waiting for their turn and hoping to win at least one game. Furthermore, some made side bets on which team would win the next hand. Charlie was sure some would have been more successful in their classes if they were studying instead of playing cards all day.

Lee and Charlie finally settled into their apartment; fall classes began. However, the couple did not have enough money to make it through the entire semester. Since Lee was about to graduate, Charlie decided to drop out and get a job to help with expenses. She worked in a city hospital in the dietary department. Charlie was good at her job but had one incident during the night shift. Her shift was responsible for mopping floors, cleaning the kitchen extensively, and emptying the grease pots. The valves had to be in a counterclockwise position to be cleaned out. However, Charlie turned the valve the wrong way, and needless to say, grease was all over the kitchen floor. Charlie was devastated, but she did not hesitate to assist with the cleanup.

The couple noticed their circle of friends changed. Some who were closest to the couple distanced themselves from Lee and Charlie. That distance forced the couple to become best friends and helped build their relationship. However, Lee was not sure about being married. Charlie went to work one morning, and when she returned, Lee was gone. Without warning, he left her alone in the apartment for two days. Charlie was not sure why he left but believed his friends knew where he was. They did not have cell phones nor beepers, and she could not contact Lee directly. Charlie called several of his friends, hoping they would tell her where Lee was, but they lied, saying they did not know where he was.

Lee finally came home but did not want to discuss why he left. Lee wanted to break up. During the argument, he told Charlie to leave. So she did. Charlie went back to Wesley's house. It was comforting being back home; however, she was sure not to mention the breakup. The breakup occurred during winter break, so going home for a while did not seem too suspicious, except for the fact that Charlie was a married woman. However, her parents did not question the visit.

Lee sent a letter to Charlie and called her long-distance. After they talked, Charlie went back to the apartment and her new life with Lee.

After graduation, Lee was hired by Phillips 66; they moved to Kansas. Lee immediately started his new career as an engineer. The couple was new in the city, and they lived with Charlie's Uncle Cee. The invitation was short-lived. Uncle Cee was naturally aggressive and did not want too many people living in his home. He was reluctant to help the newlyweds find their way in the new city.

Charlie applied for several jobs, Since she did not have a phone, she put Uncle Cee's phone number on the applications. She asked her uncle to let her know if anyone called with an offer. The Kansas Gas company called Charlie with a job offer, but her uncle neglected to notify Charlie about the call. She asked if anyone tried to contact her, and he was slow about telling her the truth. Lee and Charlie knew they were not welcome in Uncle Cee's home, so they looked for a place of their own.

Lee received his first paycheck, and Charlie found a job with an insurance company. With their combined incomes, they found a place to live and purchased furniture as well. They bought a tiny stove, refrigerator, and a sofa which doubled as a bed. The back of the couch reclined, so it was a great place to take a nap.

One morning, Charlie did not feel well, so she decided to get checked up. She went to planned parenthood, and the pregnancy test was positive. Charlie was pregnant with their first child. Charlie worked throughout the pregnancy. Since maternity leave was not an option, she quit her job when it was time for the baby to come. She wanted to be home with the new baby. Lee had a great job with good benefits. His salary would sustain the family.

During the pregnancy, their newly acquired friends visited frequently. They played cards and dominos and dabbled in a little marijuana along the way. Lee and Charlie assumed their circle of friends were trustworthy. They told their friends about their upcoming vacation. Almost immediately, the couple started receiving anonymous phone calls. Their phone would ring, but when answered, the caller would hang up. It turned out the phone calls were a precursor to an unfortunate event. Once again, their friends abandoned them. So everyone in the group of friends was suspect; someone knew who robbed them.

Once the baby came, Lee and Charlie had a family. The outsiders were no longer welcome. However, Charlie was uncomfortable being in the home alone with the baby, especially after the robbery. Lee had a co-worker who owned a house, and he told Lee a house was for sale. So Lee and Charlie bought their first home. It was a perfect two-bedroom home with a large kitchen and a living area.

It was a great starter home. However, there was one hiccup. The next-door neighbor's dog was a large German Shepherd weighing more than fifty pounds. The dog seemed fixated on the new baby who was six months old at the time. One spring day, Charlie and the baby were in the backyard. The baby was just old enough to sit up in her play chair, and she watched Charlie hang diapers on the clotheslines.

For an unknown reason, the dog started barking viciously and seemed to aim his aggression toward the baby. Charlie noticed the commotion and watched the dog, ensuring he did not attack her baby. The dog attempted to jump the fence; thank God he was too heavy to complete the jump.

Charlie grabbed her baby and went into the house. Once the baby was down for her nap, Charlie went next door to speak with her neighbor about the dog. The neighbor swore her dog was not aggressive and there were no worries. Charlie listened and allowed the neighbor to finish her statement. She told the neighbor, "If anything happens to my baby, I am going to kill that damn dog."

During the winter months, a massive snowfall covered the city. When the snow melted, that foolish dog was in Charlie's driveway, stiff as a log. Someone must have hit the dog or run over him, and he died in Charlie's driveway. Oh, no, the neighbor was going to think Charlie killed the dog on purpose. She was hysterical but never aimed any blame for the dog's death toward Charlie or her family.

Eventually, the family grew to five. Charlie was pregnant with twin girls. She had a babysitter for their first child, which worked out great. The second pregnancy was different. She was dizzy most days and could not function as expected. Charlie became a stay-at-home mom, which was great for the entire family.

Desiree stepped in to help Charlie with the twins. She moved in and taught Charlie about breastfeeding and other aspects of motherhood. The time with Desiree was great, and Charlie was happy to have her mother at her side. After the twins were born, Desiree helped with cooking, cleaning, and she showed Charlie how to feed the twins.

By placing each baby on the opposite breast, the milk produced would flow evenly on either side. The suckling of each breast created more milk for each feeding. To maintain her strength, Desiree encouraged Charlie to eat the healthy meals prepared by her mother. The time passed quickly, and Charlie realized Desiree was with her for three months.

Eventually, Desiree returned to Oklahoma. Charlie was at home until the twins turned four years old. When Charlie returned to work, she placed their daughters in Pleasant Green Baptist Church school. It was a great school, and their children loved it; everyone except the middle daughter. She cried every day when Lee dropped the girls off for school.

Charlie commuted to work via city bus from Kansas City, Kansas, across the viaduct to Missouri each day—two states separated by the Missouri River. She became friends with a group of older women who traveled together and looked out for one another. If someone ran late, they would save a seat for that person.

During one commute, there was a man aboard who was new to the route. It was a typical ride by all accounts, so Charlie was unsure what provoked the next event. The bus driver played music over the speaker system; some people read the newspaper, and others slept during the ride. Suddenly, the new guy unzipped his pants and began masturbating. It took a second for people to notice. Charlie had a bird's-eye view, and the women sitting around him shouted and screamed, drawing the bus driver's attention. The bus driver threw the guy off the bus in the middle of the commute. Charlie witnessed other weird situations on the city bus; eventually, she drove herself to work.

Lee and Charlie had a great life, a wonderful family, and enjoyed outings at different restaurants like Stevenson's Apple Farm. This outing was specifically for Lee's enjoyment as their daughters were young and only wanted hamburgers and fries for dinner. Charlie recalled the apple farm as a beautiful old farmhouse decorated with red velvet wallpaper, with a faux balcony, and paintings on the walls. The restaurant adorned the tables with white tablecloths, starched napkins, candles, and colossal drinking glasses for the frothy beer from the tap. When the waiter brought the menu to the table, Lee already knew what he wanted. He ordered green rice casserole with baked chicken, fresh apple fritters with spicy cinnamon, and flavored apple cider.

Lee had access to sporting events through his job. He was in management, and some business associates provided entertainment for the family. They frequented Royals Stadium for baseball and followed the Kansas City Chiefs at Chiefs Stadium. Lee and Charlie were in a bowling league; they were great at bowling and enjoyed their weekly outing to the bowling alley. Lee introduced bowling to their daughters, but the girls were more interested in the hotdogs and nachos from the concession stand.

FRIENDS OR NOT

Lee started his career as an engineer. There were few minorities in the office. Naturally, they gravitated toward each other. One of the secretaries was friendly with Lee and seemed to like Charlie as well. Her name was Kate. She's married and had one child with her husband, Willie. However, this couple had some internal issues that neither Lee nor Charlie knew. Willie was unfaithful and didn't care who knew about his choices. Kate pretended not to know and continued to live with and provide financial support for their family. Willie did not have a permanent job. He invested family money on numerous adventures. However, none of the investments produced any income. For example, Willie went into business with four friends. Each partner invested twenty thousand dollars in a record store. He talked Kate into getting the money from her 401(k) to match his friends' contribution. They acquired a building and hired people to work in the store. Willie was supposed to manage the store while keeping the books for possible audits. However, he was not reliable; he was missing in action most days.

Willie was irresponsible and lived a relaxed life. Kate supported the family while he imbibed and smoked marijuana. During this time, smoking marijuana was acceptable, and most enjoyed engaging in the activity. But those with responsibilities and families to care for should've been more reliable. Some worked during the week and saved the partying for the weekend. Willie lived for the party and was instrumental in pushing his lifestyle on others in his purview. He always had an idea about making money but wasn't willing to perform labor to produce an income. The record store went bankrupt, and the closing of the business was primarily Willie's fault. He never seemed down about losing the investment money or causing his friends to lose out as well. He was a party boy and continued the lifestyle for many years.

Kate befriended Charlie. She was older and had a great career. Kate's little girl was a few months old, and Charlie was pregnant and due to deliver soon, so she and Kate had something in common. Kate shared maternity clothes with Charlie and helped her become familiar with sites around the city. However, the dynamics between the ladies shifted. Lee spent his lunch hour at home with Charlie. They ate lunch together, and Lee would return to work confident that Charlie would be okay for the rest of the afternoon. However, Kate started coming over for lunch, sometimes beating Lee to the apartment and wanting to be included in Charlie and Lee's time together. For some reason, Lee thought it was okay for Kate to be in the apartment almost daily. Charlie became suspicious of Kate and Lee's possible attraction for each other. She contemplated asking Lee about the situation with Kate but was hesitant to broach the subject.

ANOTHER PARTY

One day, when picking up the baby from the babysitter, Charlie mentioned her despair about Lee and Kate. She told the babysitter how she felt and that she wasn't sure how to react. The babysitter was a much older woman. She advised that Charlie shouldn't sit back and allow anyone to affect her marriage. Charlie confronted Lee and Kate. Lee thought it was funny that Charlie was jealous, and Kate seemed taken aback when Charlie showed up on her porch and threatened to kick her ass if she didn't leave Lee alone. The confrontation caused some discomfort for Lee and Kate as they still worked together. However, Charlie didn't care. She just wanted her husband and their marriage to work. Kate backed off. Charlie missed their friendship but couldn't allow anyone to cause problems in her marriage.

Lee and his best friend Ken attended primary school through college together. And they moved to Kansas around the same time. Ken thought all women wanted to be with him and was under the impression that he and Carrol would automatically connect because of Lee and Charlie's relationship. Ken tried to force his affection on Carrol, but she wasn't interested. Once he realized Carrol didn't want to be with him, his attitude toward Charlie changed. He was rude and sometimes verbally abusive toward her. Ken approached Charlie and wanted her to make Carrol be with him. When Charlie refused, he tried to intimidate her. Charlie stood her ground and cursed Ken out in the student union. Lee didn't defend Charlie, and maybe it was for the best. Lee and Charlie's relationship was new, so his loyalty was still with Ken. But that scenario changed as Lee and Charlie's relationship evolved, and Lee cut off his friendship with Ken.

Ken was a womanizer. He dated two different women at the same time. Both ladies lived in his hometown and knew each other but were not aware that Ken was sexually involved with both ladies. The ladies became pregnant, and their babies were born months apart. Somehow, Ken kept the ladies apart and talked each of them into moving to Kansas. One lady came to visit Ken but returned to her mother's home. Ken's living arrangement didn't meet her expectations, so she broke up with him.

The other lady came to visit and stayed. She already had two children and was responsible for watching her mother's seven other children while she worked and sold Amway products part-time. The other lady was called Monique. Her first child was from a previous relationship, and Ken was the father of the second child. She and Ken eventually married and formed a family together. During their marriage, Ken cheated with the upstairs neighbor. While Monique worked, the neighbor and Ken were together during the day. Somehow, Monique found out about the affair but kept the information to herself. Charlie and Monique were good friends and frequented nightclubs together. Monique's birthday was coming up, and she and Charlie went out for the night. While in the lounge, the party was great.

The live band, food, and the crowd made her birthday celebration even better. Until Monique recognized Ken's voice from across the room, she stood up and located him in the group. Monique went outside and came back into the club. She walked directly to Ken's table and confronted him. The upstairs neighbor was there as well. She made the mistake of speaking up in Ken's defense. Monique pulled a beer bottle from beneath her dress and hit the neighbor across her forehead. Her forehead immediately began to swell. Ken tried to intervene, but Monique told Ken to "shut the fuck up." Security noticed the commotion and walked Monique out of the club. The security team warned her she would be arrested; she didn't care. She accomplished her goal, so she told security to go ahead, "call the police." the security guard told Monique to leave and that she couldn't come back to the club again.

In the meantime, Charlie was sitting in her car, not sure if she should wait or leave. Monique finally came to the car and told Charlie, "Let's get out of here." Charlie hit the gas and talked to

Monique about the events of the night. Monique asked Charlie to take her to the bus station. "I've got to get out of here." Between the fights and the cheating, Ken and Monique managed to have three additional children. Once Monique was settled back in their hometown, her mother drove to Kansas to pick up the children. Eventually, Ken moved on and made his home in Mississippi with the upstairs neighbor.

THE INSURANCE
COMPANY

Charlie worked as a cashier at an insurance company. She met and became friends with several coworkers. The group consisted of several twentysomethings—all women, and most of them were young mothers. There was one co-worker who was a talented artist. She was a cashier but loved fashion and the arts. Her name was Janice. She had a hair show and invited her co-workers to participate in the show. Charlie fit in, as she already wore braids and loved fashion as well. Janice tried to influence the group of friends to attend church with her and spend time with her family. Janice had several sisters who always found a reason to party. So the group of friends bonded over food and drinks.

There was another co-worker named Ardelia. She smoked marijuana and drank liquor daily. Her demeanor was suspect, as she slept at her desk and protested if anyone tried to wake her. That included Mr. Alexander, her boss. Charlie believes Mr. Alexander knew Ardelia's plight, but he did not fire her for some reason. She was married to her high school sweetheart, Reggie. They had two children together. Reggie was a drug dealer. He slept during the day and partied most nights. Ardelia wasn't happy in the relationship. She knew Reggie was a womanizer. He was bold and indifferent and wasn't concerned that others knew about his lifestyle.

Charlie was on a smoke break. She was sitting in front of a large picture window on the fifth floor of the insurance company. As she gazed out of the window, she noticed a car at the traffic light attempting a left-hand turn. During the turn, another vehicle approached and broadsided the turning vehicle. The oncoming vehicle's impact caused the driver's ejection. She sat in the driver's seat, but her body exited through the front passenger window. The lady was Black, but her skin turned an ash-gray shade when her body hit the pavement. That may have been when her blood stopped circulating. Charlie believes she died upon impact.

Charlie asked a co-worker to call the police and report the accident. The operator asked to speak to the person who witnessed the incident. Therefore, Charlie talked to the operator. She had the presence of mind to describe the accident and gave directions to the location of the wreck. It seemed like time stopped as onlookers waited for the police and the ambulance to arrive. Charlie never forgot this accident, mainly because there was a reminder she saw daily. The glass and pieces of the car laid in the roadway for weeks after the wreck. The victim's blood was visible until the next rain shower or storm hit the city. After a while, some became aware the victim was an employee who worked in the hotel next door to the insurance company. She worked in food services and had most likely helped during events such as Christmas or Thanksgiving dinners sponsored by the insurance company in previous years. The company sent flowers and condolences to the victim's family.

Doris is another friend who worked at the insurance company. She was acholic, but no one knew it. One day, Charlie asked if anyone had any gum. Doris told Charlie to look in her purse; she had some Juicy Fruit gum. Charlie opened Doris's bag, and there it was, big as life, a flask nestled between the lotion and tissues in Doris's handbag. Charlie looked at Doris and asked her about the flask. Doris just smiled at Charlie and continued with her work.

Doris's mother passed, and her co-workers attended the funeral. In Black people's tradition, they brought food and flowers and took the items to the family home. Upon arrival, they heard someone shrieking, bellowing, screaming to the top of their lungs. It was Doris. She was inebriated, out of her mind with grief. The co-workers dropped the items off and continued the trip over to the church. They sat together in the church with a full view of those entering the services for the final viewing.

Doris stumbled as she walked down the aisle to her seat. Those sounds continued, and before they knew it, Doris ran to her mother and landed inside the casket on top of her mother's body. The funeral directors quickly removed Doris from the coffin and walked her outside. Doris was embarrassed because of her actions during the funeral. She was never seen by her co-workers again. They wondered why Doris's sister seemed distant. She didn't appear concerned by Doris's display. Their relationship was fractured because of Doris's drinking. However, Charlie managed to visit Doris once more. She lived in a one-bedroom apartment alone. She was still drinking and trying to accept her mother's death.

THE BABYSITTER

Charlie needed a babysitter for her little girl. While searching the local newspaper, she came across an ad for a babysitting service. Charlie met with the owner. Her name was Earnestine. They became fast friends. It seems as if they already knew each other. They had a lot in common, and Earnestine's family members welcomed Charlie and Lee with open arms. Earnestine was a great sitter. Charlie never worried about her baby while she was in Earnestine's care. They invited Charlie and Lee over for a weekend get-together. At the time, partaking in a little marijuana now and then was recreational. No harm, no file. Since Charlie and Lee partied in the same style as Earnestine, they blended in well. The group played cards and dominos into the wee hours of the night. There were never any problems among the families. Between the barbecue ribs and chicken Earnestine's husband Phil cooked on the grill, it was just games, music, and fun. If someone had a birthday or a wedding anniversary, there was always a reason to have a party.

Lee and Charlie traveled from Kansas City, Kansas, to Dallas, Texas, to celebrate the New Year. There was a change in the weather; snow and ice plummeted the highway. The streets were so bad; they were glad about purchasing the small Volkswagen Rabbit just in time for the trip. The car was perfect for the icy roads. The trip was exciting for their daughter, who was small but enjoyed traveling. As long as she had food and toys to play with, she was happy. It was a long trip between Dallas, Texas, and Kansas City, Kansas. However, the family made it home safely with minimal stops except to purchase gas and to stretch their legs.

The family embarked on a vacation to New Orleans. They had a great time attending the World's Fair. They stayed at the Avenue

Plaza Hotel on St. Charles Street, which was their favorite place to stay when in New Orleans. Since Lee and Charlie vacationed in New Orleans frequently, they knew the city well and had specific locations to visit when in town. They wanted to see the cemetery on Girod Street. The graveyard was famous, as several movie directors included the site in movies over the years. The attraction for Lee's family was the above-ground graves. It was scary and exciting because of the backstory of each burial site. According to tradition, the Gates of Guinee is famous; it is the ingress to the voodoo underbelly. Lee and Charlie always enjoyed this city. Great food, atmosphere, and many famous tourist attractions.

WESLEY AND DESIREE

Charlie was married, the mother of three children, and she was devoted to her immediate family; she always cared for her parents. They lived in Oklahoma and visited Charlie and her family often. Charlie and her father shared a close relationship, but she was not as close to her mother, as one would think. Charlie was a daddy's girl, and Desiree resented their relationship.

Her son left home early and joined the army. Their relationship was tenuous at best. As Iverson matured and became a man in his own right, he related more to Wesley and thought of him as a dad. A few years later, Charlie found a letter addressed to Wesley; it was from Iverson. He stated,

> I wanted to take this opportunity to tell you how much I appreciate having you for my father. I know I don't tell you enough, but I do love you. Proud to be your son.
>
> Iverson

Charlie found proof that Iverson loved Wesley as his father. Desiree and Iverson never reached the point of a loving mother-son relationship. Charlie thought both wanted more from each other but did not know how to express their desire.

Desiree was selfish and somehow unaware of her position in life. Her parenting seemed like a competition instead of mothering. She confided in Ruth by sharing intimate details about her marriage. Ruth did not just listen to Desiree; she expressed her disdain for Wesley to his face.

Charlie recalled one family fight that could have gone too far. As usual, Wesley and Desiree were arguing, but this time, Ruth was in the house. Charlie was there but knew not to involve herself in the fight. She was in her bedroom with the door closed; however, she could hear the entire kerfuffle. She heard loud voices, doors slamming, and people cursing.

Ruth heard about Desiree's upset in a previous conversation and wanted to defend her mother this time. She reared up to Wesley, stating in a loud voice, "You better leave my mother alone!"

Wesley was furious and already extremely upset. When Ruth inserted herself into the argument, he asked, "What are you doing?" He raised his voice and threatened Ruth by saying, "I will knock you through that wall!"

Charlie could not hide any longer. She had to stop the fight before Wesley physically hurt someone. Wesley and Ruth were within inches of a physical confrontation. He stood near the linen closet in the hallway, and Ruth was a few feet away from him. Wesley's fists were in position as if he wanted to fight. Ruth seemed eager for a possible fight with Wesley. She thought she could fight anyone, and that included men. Screaming to the top of her lungs, Charlie told Wesley and Ruth, "Just stop! Just stop it!" Charlie's words calmed the rage between her father and sister.

Ruth eventually walked away, and Wesley looked at Charlie, seemly embarrassed about his behavior. He went into the master bedroom and closed the door. It was not the first instance where those two were at each other's throats. Desiree was in the middle each time, pitting one family member against the other.

Desiree tried to use her magic on Iverson, but he never took the bait. He always defended Wesley and told Desiree she was wasting her time trying to include him in the family drama. Wesley had his demons but kept them at bay when Charlie was involved. He was passionate and loving but never let people in until they earned his trust.

Wesley could not trust Desiree or Ruth. They were the two individuals who caused the upset in the household. Wesley asked Desiree to spend more time with him. Desiree did not comply with his simple requests. She occupied her time by trapping Ruth into shopping trips and garage sales on Saturday mornings. Anything to frustrate Wesley; and she did not display remorse for upsetting her husband.

Wesley's demons were noticeable, but he had a way of hiding them in plain sight. When his demons reared their ugly heads, Wesley remained in his room with the door shut. It seemed like he was not home most times because he seldom ventured from his inner sanctum. He slept, ate, read, and listened to preaching albums in that room. Few had access to the room, and at times, the rule applied to Charlie.

Desiree slept in Charlie's room. She had twin beds, so it was easy for Desiree to slip into the twin bed closest to the bedroom door. Wesley and Desiree slept in separate rooms because he snored loudly and interrupted Desiree's sleep. Somehow, Desiree and Charlie switched beds one night. Wesley opened the bedroom door and grabbed Charlie's toes. She fell asleep in Desiree's bed. She woke up and asked Wesley, "Daddy, what do you want?"

Wesley was shocked to find Charlie in Desiree's bed. He immediately closed the door and vanished into the night. Later, Charlie realized Wesley wanted to be with Desiree, and she knew it. She was not sure how she switched beds with Charlie, but Desiree did not go into Wesley's room that night.

Some interactions between Wesley and Desiree were confusing to Charlie. She did not know how married couples should relate to one another but was savvy enough to know their example of love was not what she wanted in her life. Charlie heard how they met and how they partied together before they married. During that time, the big band sound was the music played in the nightclubs. Wesley and Desiree cut a rug and enjoyed that time together. However, as they aged and became involved in the church, the fun waned. At least, that is what Charlie witnessed.

Some clergy in the COGIC church pretend they were not sexual beings. That misnomer is believed by some now. Charlie's generation thought that sexual thoughts and intercourse were against God's plan for their life. If someone became sexually active and ended up pregnant, they had to get married. Alternatively, the woman involved would be shunned and shamed, similar to having a large red X on her back.

A family friend's daughter became pregnant. They were members of a large congregation with a membership of five hundred people, so the audience was filled. To keep his reputation intact, he forced her to stand in front of the church and apologize to everyone for being pregnant. Charlie heard the story about the family friend forcing his daughter to apologize to the church. She did not think it was fair or something a parent should do to their child.

Charlie spoke up about the situation, and Wesley was upset with her. First of all, she was not an adult, and she was speaking against something a preacher did. He sent Charlie to her room. In those days, people did not speak against a preacher. Charlie thought deeply about the situation and theorized, "The sin is in the fornication. The pregnancy is a gift from God." Some clergy had extramarital relationships and fathered children out of wedlock. Since most were afraid to speak up about the shenanigans, it was possible to keep their actions top secret.

A FAMILY FRIEND

It's incredible how some choose to live. The preacher who embarrassed his daughter in front of the congregation had an affair with his wife's live-in nurse. His name was Rev. Glasscock. While judging his daughter, he slept with the nurse as his wife lay sick. The affair was exposed, and some turned their backs on the preacher. After all, he was a fornicator and a hypocrite. Rev. Glasscock had eleven children with his wife. She was a missionary in the church and volunteered in the community. The upheaval wasn't easy to live down. The church gossip would be hurtful, but something of this magnitude would always be a topic for discussion. Rev. Glasscock left the church and his family. He had a full-blown relationship with the nurse, who happened to be a white lady.

One night, there was a knock on the door of the Reiss home. It was Rev. Glasscock and his companion. He drove long-distance to visit Rev. Reiss. Rev. Glasscock was banging on the front door and calling Rev. Reiss's name out loud.

"Rev., open the door!"

However, Wesley did not open the door for his longtime friend. He could not allow this guy to bring a white woman into his home. After all, races didn't mix freely during those days. So having someone of a different race in your family home was unfamiliar. Wesley could not associate with Rev. Glasscock because the church shunned him. Once he realized that Wesley would not open the door, Rev. Glasscock eventually left their home. That was probably the last time Rev. Glasscock tried to contact Wesley. Wesley talked with Charlie about the Glasscock family situation. He told Charlie that he was sorry for being angry with her for expressing her opinion and apologized for punishing her. Wesley was embarrassed because of his friend's actions, as interracial relationships were not acceptable. It wasn't easy to describe how Wesley felt, but Charlie knew he loved her, and that was all that mattered.

Wesley had a friend who happened to be blind. He was an accomplished organist and soloist in the church. His name was Rev. Daniels. He was known worldwide, and he traveled extensively displaying his craft. Somehow, Wesley and Rev. Daniels became friends. When Rev. Daniels was in town, he visited the Reiss home many times. He loved Charlie, and she enjoyed making him guess who she was. Charlie didn't realize it, but Rev. Daniels always knew when she was around. He was blind but knew people by smell and other senses. So it was funny watching Charlie think she tricked Rev. Daniels once again. One evening after church, Rev. Daniels was still sitting at the organ. Charlie tiptoed over to him, and the moment she raised herself upon the organ platform, he called her name. She was so tickled all she could do was laugh out loud, and he joined in the fun. He was a nice gentleman and showed everyone that his disability was a gift from God. When Rev. Daniels played the organ, he rocked side to side and played the most beautiful melodies anyone ever heard. His musical prowess was great for Desiree, and she loved playing music with him during church. He was one person who loved the entire family.

Wesley was a moral man. He had integrity and believed in teaching Charlie a lesson in Christian values. Charlie accompanied Wesley to the grocery store to pick up food for the week. The cashier rang up their groceries. The total bill was less than fifty dollars. When Wesley paid the bill, he gave the cashier fifty dollars cash. The cashier gave him forty dollars back. Charlie was excited to see the mistake and thought Wesley should have taken the money. However, Wesley told Charlie, "No, that's not how we operate. The right thing to do was point out the mistake." He did just that. Wesley counted the money back to the cashier. The lesson; stealing in any form is not acceptable. Charlie always remembered that day and incorporated Wesley's beliefs into her lifestyle.

In contrast, Wesley was fiercely protective of his family. Anyone who thought they could attack the Reiss family was mistaken. Wesley took his grandchildren to the hospital on a mission trip. He taught them about visiting the sick and showing other people humility and concern. However, there was an older man sitting in the waiting room of the hospital. For some reason, he took an attack on Wesley's grandchildren and said they were a bunch of niggas keeping up all that noise. Wesley heard the commotion and politely excused the children from the area. He approached the older man and told him what would happen if he ever called anyone else a nigga. The man apologized to the children. That day marked some of those children's first encounter with racism. Wesley was experienced and knew how to deal with such people.

THE FINALE

Is it possible for a God-fearing man to consent to the ebbs and flows of everyday life? After all, he was a preacher, and he was well-known in the community. Wesley was called on to preside over numerous events. If there was a death or marriage approaching, Wesley was ready to serve. Are people who choose to live a particular lifestyle expected to ignore their innermost needs and continue to mentor and console others? So many questions and so few answers. Wesley had problems but did not succeed in satisfying the longing for a resolve.

Wesley's anxiety stemmed from his childhood. Remember, he was black, male, and fatherless. He did not have a mentor to shape his thoughts or to guide him. Yes, Liz was there, but she could not teach him about manhood. His stepfather was a horrible example of what a man should aspire to become.

Some people in the city knew Mister for his disdain for most. He kept his demons under wraps until Liz agreed to be his wife. She thought he would help raise her sons. However, she was mistaken. He needed a maid, someone to slop the hogs and feed the chickens. Liz and her sons fit the bill. They lived in his house, but it was not home. Wesley's upbringing was not loving, comforting, nor a welcoming existence. However, they had no other choice. A single black woman with four sons in tow was not an invitation readily accepted. Mister did his level best to discourage anyone from feeling comfortable in his house. And that line of thinking was aimed at four boys he refused to love.

Most kept their emotions quiet and did not easily display affection. The approach was to survive until daybreak hit the horizon, then realize God allowed them to fight another day. Black men worked their owners' fields, while the women cooked in white people's kitchen and took care of the boss's children. Some worked as live-in maids. They lived in the servant's quarters and were available for their boss's every whim. Therefore, they were gone weeks at a time, leaving their own children's care to others.

The circumstances under which Wesley grow helped create that tuff exterior exhibited to those around him. Wesley was a standup guy. If he needed to defend or protect someone, you could depend on him. He was involved with unsavory scoundrels, and again, Wesley had to fight to establish himself as a man. That's what he knew, and that's how he lived as a young man.

Wesley was a man of God; he sincerely believed in the principles of Christianity. His faith was an example of someone who knew God for himself; there was no other way to survive this life. One had to live according to the teaching of the Gospel.

Wesley was not highly educated but self-taught in most aspects of life. He dedicated himself to studying God's Word and listened to sermons by well-known Gospel preachers. Wesley listened to Rev. C. L. Franklin and Bishop G. E. Patterson from Memphis, Tennessee. In the wee hours of the night, Charlie could hear Wesley practicing sermons. He wrote his sermons out on a yellow business pad and translated them into Gospel preaching as the Holy Spirit directed.

Regardless of his mistakes, sins, and other negatives, Wesley had a call on his life. He may have mishandled the anointing by not following the instructions to the letter. Nevertheless, God used him to persuade hundreds to follow Christ. Jesus gives us a choice as he will not force himself on anyone, leaving room for them to make decisions for themselves.

Wesley was not outwardly affectionate; he loved deeply but did not display his love for others to weigh. He had his way of showing love for Charlie. It could have been felt by a glance of approval or correction if needed. His eyes were bright and expressive, and that smile was his trademark. He had a broad smile that showed his heritage.

Wesley's mother, Liz, was mixed with Cherokee Indian, and she passed some features of that tribe to her sons. The high cheekbones exhibited in Wesley's smile created his trademark. Wesley came from a meager beginning and entered an adult life full of consternation. His happiness was measured and possibly overshadowed by outside sources. He was born with the weight of the world on his shoulders. He was black, male, and fatherless.

His parents were the offspring of slaves living in the dust bowl of the Midwest. They had little to offer their children as some of what they endured growing up was not up for discussion. Liz was married at the age of fourteen, the mother of four by the age of twenty, and eventually widowed by twenty-nine. She had to grow up quickly as her mother passed during the birth of her little sister.

Liz had to pick up where her mother left off. She attended school but did not finish elementary school. Liz babysat her younger sister while cooking and cleaning their home. Liz loved to read, and by reading, she knew what was happening in her town and around the world. She was intrigued by all subject matter and enhanced her vocabulary through reading. She had limited formal education but taught her sons to be hardworking people.

There is limited knowledge about Wesley's father. He died at an early age, and that is where his background stops. Therefore, Wesley discovered his destiny through circumstance. Wesley lost his battle with cancer in the spring of 1999. However, he lost his zest for life long before cancer crept in and suffocated him. The lineage continues.

ABOUT THE AUTHOR

Charlotte Reece Brown has a thirty-year career in the engineering industry; she was afforded numerous opportunities in editing and writing documents and procedures within that field. One of Charlotte's first articles was published in the *Houston Chronicle Newspaper*. Subject matter was about allowing prayers to continue within the public school systems. While attending classes at the University of Phoenix, the writer within Charlotte emerged. Therefore, writing *Daddy's Dying: There Is No Will* already existed in her spirit. Charlotte is the mother of twin daughters; her oldest daughter is a lawyer and mother of seven. Charlotte has been married to her college sweetheart for forty-six years.

ABOUT THE ARTIST

She is a talented artist who was gracious in illustrating the works for this book. JoieB's involvement in the arts spanned throughout her life. She is a dancer-choreographer and has participated in several stage plays. In addition, she has a passion for individuals on the Autism Spectrum. She found her calling. JoieB is devoted to helping others while opening her heart to receive love from those she assists.

9 781638 149309